EXHIBITING OURSELVES

For Stella, Becky and Sally, whose very existence keeps me going.

Published by Artmonsky Arts
Flat 1, 27 Henrietta Street
London WC2E 8NA
www.ruthartmonsky.com
ruthartmonsky@yahoo.co.uk
Tel. 020 7240 8774

Text © Ruth Artmonsky 2014

ISBN 978-0-9573875-4-6

Designed by David Preston Studio
www.davidprestonstudio.com

Printed in England by Northend Creative Print
Solutions, Clyde Road, Heeley, Sheffield, S8 0TZ

Acknowledgements
The main resource for this book has been my own
design library and ephemera collection, but I would
like to give special thanks to Helen Marvin and David
Bell at the Imperial War Museum Photographic
Archive for their help with the 'Propaganda
Exhibition' section and to Evelyn Watson, archivist at
RSA for her help on all matters related to the Society.
I not only thank my book designer, David Preston,
for his imaginative design of the book but also for his
additive interest in it and patience in its collation.

Front and back cover illustrations: Andrew
Renton. **Following page:** Gordon Cullen's
illustration of the Royal Festival Hall terraces.

Ruth Artmonsky

EXHIBITING OURSELVES

Fifty Years of British Exhibition Design

CONTENTS

'The exhibition designer works in a floodlit hinterland between the elegant mansions of the architects and the gayer dwellings of the commercial artists. He practices a craft which is unable to boast a single textbook or a sustained course of technical instruction. The exhibition designer is a hybrid, parented by architects, suckled by designers, and reared in the violent atmosphere of the circus, disturbed by the raucous shouts of the travelling salesman.'

Misha Black, 1948

'The exhibitioneers have found that it takes more than pictures, models and replicas to hold the imagination of the public, who by the time they have been in the show for half an hour are beginning to feel bemused and punch-drunk. Physical and emotional fatigue are so great in these exhibitions that while the public is in a sense denuded of its normal defenses and critical faculties and therefore receptive to any plausible notion, they are also so numbed that special effects must be made to get them to take notice of what is before them.'

James Boswell, 1947

'The designer as a nameable entity came on the exhibition scene some time after the First World War. He inherited on the one hand a chaotic if sometimes sumptuous tradition stretching right back to 1851, and, on the other, our glorious island tradition of the church bazaar; neighing vicars armed with faith, hope and drawing pins.'

Milner Gray, 1952

INTRODUCTION

Exhibition Design as a field worthy of specific research, only really began to appeal to me when I was writing 'Showing Off', a book on retail store display and advertising, albeit I had been aware of the considerable body of enthusiasts for the subject, particularly the collectors searching for their various holy grails – an entrance ticket to the Great Exhibition, commemorative exhibition stamps, or any trinket sold during the Festival of Britain with Abram Games' head of Britannia upon it.

It was when preparing 'Showing Off' and experiencing difficulty drawing a line between a display for a shop window and one for an exhibition, that I began to shift my focus of interest to the latter. This was aided by my daily sighting of two spikey Ernest Day chairs for the Festival of Britain, bought at the time and now in front of one of my windows, and a watercolour sketch of a preliminary plan for the Festival, emanating from Hugh Casson's office, now on my wall.

'Exhibiting Ourselves' takes a look at the more earthy, every-day exhibitions as well as the grander affairs. It is a contribution to a subject not only of interest to the collector or to the social historian, but to anybody interested in the development of the design profession in this country.

SHARP'S
AT
WEMBLEY - 1925.

THE TALK OF THE EXHIBITION

SHARP'S
SUPER-KREEM
TOFFEE

EXHIBITION
VENUES

The White City at Shepherd's Bush and Wembley were the two main London sites that were virgin territory, as it were, upon which grandiose exhibition pavilions were constructed, used for a time for shows, but eventually converted to general commercial use or just pulled down.

The White City had been just scrubland before it was developed to mount the Franco-British Exhibition in 1908, which ensued from the Entente Cordiale, signed in 1904. The site acquired its name from the exhibition buildings, which were all painted white. The task of creating the exhibition was given to Imre Kiralfy, who brought in his son, Charles, as general manager, and his son, Albert, as works director. Kiralfy was already flexing his muscles at Olympia and Earls Court. He involved some sixteen architects in the building of the exhibition pavilions and the stadium, which was constructed alongside, for the Olympic Games. Hot on the heels of the Franco-British Exhibition, the White City was to be used for a number of similar shows – the Japan-British Exhibition of 1910, the Latin Exhibition of 1913, and the Anglo-American Exhibition of 1914. The grounds were adapted to the specific needs of each, with the occasional new pavilion being built.

The White City was also the original base for the British Industries Fair, which, throughout the 1920s were run both there and at Olympia, until, in the late 1930s, it transferred to Olympia and Earls Court. Over the years, the White City became better known as a sporting venue, rather than as an exhibition site – for greyhound racing, athletics and football. By the 1930s part of the site was taken over by Hammersmith Council for housing, and, much of the rest, was later developed by the BBC.

As Olympia and Earls Court were to have parallel histories, so were Wembley and the White City. Both were established for a specific exhibition, and both

Previous spread: British Empire Exhibition, Wembley, 1924. **Left:** Franco-British Exhibition, White City, 1908. **Opposite:** New Empire Hall, Olympia, 1930 (architect, Joseph Emberton).

eventually shifted their focus of activity from exhibitions to sport. In 1921 Wembley was a greenfield site to be developed specifically for the British Empire Exhibition of 1924–5. As the White City had its Olympic Stadium, Wembley was to have its Football Stadium, with the Football Association's Cup Final being played there during the Exhibition. In fact the British Empire Exhibition was to be the only one held on the original site, for when it closed the pavilions were either pulled down, transported to other sites, or converted for commercial use. The Stadium continued to be used for national and international football and speedway, along with swimming at the nearby Empire Pool. It was not until 1970 that the Conference Centre was built, holding, for a time, such probably under-designed exhibitions as those for the British Philatelic Society.

Wembley and the White City were relatively easy sites to develop for exhibitions being largely flat. When the Scots were allocated parkland for their own Empire Exhibition in 1938, they had the challenge of constructing it around a hill at Bellahouston, which although having level ground on three sides was wooded on the fourth. Its catalogue bragged of the solution:

Here the genius of the presiding architect has wedded the palaces and pavilions to the charm of the hill and the trees...

The architect, Tait, not only made use of the hill, but flaunted it, making it the focus of the exhibition by mounting on it a 300ft tower with staircase, and having water cascading down the hillside.

Weather conditions were a major factor when developing large sites for exhibitions, as was to be experienced on the South Bank for the Festival of Britain. Obviously it was unpleasant for visitors to circulate, in bad weather, between the pavilions, which were such a feature of many of the exhibitions held in the first half of the 20th century; but weather was obviously a considerable challenge in the construction and maintenance of the buildings. From the British Empire Exhibition, where the

Pageant of the Empire had to be delayed a week because of rain, to Tait's problems with high winds whipping his tower, to the Festival of Britain's dreary rain soaked construction site, weather was always a feature to be factored in for outdoor sited exhibitions. Of course it was ever present at the many agricultural shows, where occasionally exhibition tents would be blown down by high winds. Such problems obviously made it preferable to hold exhibitions in permanent buildings.

Olympia and Earls Court have been the two most important buildings in London used as exhibition venues. Olympia first opened its doors in 1886 with a circus (the Paris Hippodrome Circus) and would continue, for some eighty years to have an annual circus (Bertram Mills) showing there from 1920 to 1965. Olympia started out as a place of entertainment, with increasingly lavish shows mounted there by the impresario Imre Kiralfy. It was, in fact, one, General Barnaby, needing more room for his military tournament, previously held at the Agricultural Hall in Islington, that prompted the building of Olympia in the first place. The land was purchased for this purpose in the 1860s and the Great Hall, later to be known as the Grand Hall, was designed by Henry Coe. The building, set in gardens, had a roof over 100ft high, consisting of some 2,500 sheets of glass. Over the years Olympia expanded, a New Hall, which became known as the National Hall being added in 1923, with Joseph Emberton's grand art deco Empire Hall being added in 1929.

Below: Earls Court Exhibition, showing the Western Gardens and Great Wheel, 1904.
Opposite: Earls Court Exhibition building, 1938 (architect, C. Howard Crane).

Earls Court Exhibition. 1904.

The Western Gardens and Great Wheel.

Along with Kiralfy's early razzamatazz, the circuses, tournaments, the dog and horse shows, Olympia became the home of long running trade exhibitions – the motor show, the boat show, Radiolympia, Daily Mail's Ideal Home Exhibition and the British Industries Fairs. In fact it was the Board of Trade's interest in the last that triggered the building of the Empire Hall. Olympia claimed the first motor show and one of the first aeronautical exhibitions in the early years of the 20th century; and, in the late 1950s, was to hold the first computer exhibition.

Earls Court had a similar, but rather more checkered history. Its rather awkward triangular site, lying between railway lines, had been owned by the Earl of Zetland – hence its name. John Robinson Whitley

had the idea to develop the site for entertainment, and had a one storey building constructed in 1887. Imre Kiralfy, already operating at Olympia, took a lease on the building, and, as at Olympia, mounted extravaganza, including a number of international exhibitions, until WWI, when it was used by the government. Unlike Olympia it did not mount trade exhibitions until the London Passenger Transport Board became the site's freeholder and leased the building to largely American investors – the Earls Court Ltd. A new Exhibition Hall, designed by an American architect, C. Howard Crane, was built in the late 1930s, which, with a ground and upper floor, could hold up to four exhibitions simultaneously. So attractive was the new building that a number of exhibitions that had previously been held at Olympia

Left: 'The Highway Code' exhibition, Charing Cross Underground Station, 1937 (designer, Hans Schleger).
Right: 'British Art in Industry' exhibition, showing masking of the Royal Academy rooms, 1935.

now transferred to Earls Court, as the motor show, the boat show and the Ideal Home Exhibition. As a postscript, it is perhaps poignant that Olympia and Earls Court, which had been competitive sites for so many years, were to be merged in the 1970s to form Jeffrey Stirling's ECO (Earls Court & Olympia Co.).

Various other London sites were used for exhibitions from time to time, as the Royal Agricultural Hall in Islington, built in 1862, which was originally intended largely for agricultural shows. The Royal Horticultural Halls, around Vincent Square, were built at the turn of the century and extended in the 1930s. Each new exhibition building tended to claim itself as being the largest, highest, grandest of its time. The Dorland Hall is occasionally mentioned as a venue, and was used, perhaps most frequently during WWII, for such iconic Ministry of Information exhibitions as Milner Gray's 'America Marches'.

Other sites occasionally used were Westminster Hall, where designers felt it necessary to completely mask the ornate decoration in order to mount 'modern' shows; and the Tea Centre, which provided 'a gay fascia to the more austere end of Regent Street'. Here, with Misha Black as display consultant, they held exhibitions mainly relating to tea and tea drinking – or, as *Design* describe it, 'opening its doors to all who want to show good designs and all who want to see it'.

'If to the question "where is such and such an exhibition to be held?" one gets the answer "at the Tea Centre", it is today almost a guarantee that this will be a stimulating exhibition.'

And then there was Charing Cross Underground Station, to which visitors flocked in the war years, the Ministry of Information holding many of its most important exhibitions there. Today its considerable empty passageways, containing the odd tramp sleeping rough, seem to cry out to be made use of again, possibly for something similar, although this seems unlikely with government messages so easily getting across by electronic means.

On the whole, art galleries seem to have been reluctant to act as venues for any exhibitions other than those of 'fine' art, and certainly not for showing off massed produced products (the sort of things the general public buys). The Whitechapel Gallery, in the East End, is recorded as mounting an 'engineering' exhibition as early as 1912, and a 'Munitions of War and Allied Industries' one in 1918, but beyond that

Edward McKnight Kauffer poster for 'Schools Exhibition' at Dorland Hall, 1938.

19

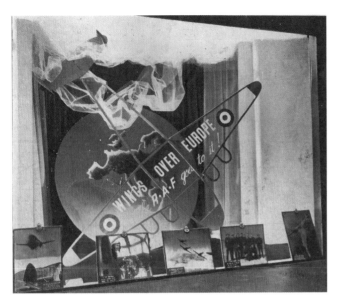

Ministry of Information 'Wings Over Europe' wartime shop window display scheme, 1940, Galleries Lafayette.

To put on the exhibition fake ceilings and plaster walls had to be constructed at the considerable expense of £10,000.

Although the Royal Scottish Museum appears to have been positive about its use for 'Enterprise Scotland' in 1947, the V&A seems to have been altogether more ambivalent about its use, in the previous year, for the first major post-war exhibition, and the first important exhibition of the newly formed Council of Industrial Design – 'Britain Can Make It' (BCMI). Actually, in the early years of the 20th century the V&A were seemingly quite happy, working along with both the Board of Trade and the British Institute of Industrial Art, to mount the odd exhibition of a not dissimilar nature as the 1929 'British Industrial Art for the Slender Purse'; and, earlier, through the latter part of the 19th century had even made its rooms available for trade fairs.

BCMI was to be a rather different story. At the end of WWII, Leigh Ashton, then the Director of the V&A, was virtually sitting in an empty gallery (its contents having been removed for safe keeping during the war); he could be described as surveying a blank canvas with the power to show what he wanted to show in any place where he wanted to place it, and in whatever way he chose. Here is not the place to detail the V&A's uneasy history with such governmental bodies as the British Institute of Industrial Art, the Council for Art & Industry, and, the then new Council of Industrial Design; nor to tell of Ashton's rivalry with Kenneth Clark at the

seem to have stayed with 'art' until post-WWII, when, in 1956, they mounted 'Setting up Home for Bill and Betty, an East End couple with a budget of £50'!

Even when Burlington House saw some kudos in combining with the Royal Society of Arts for the 'Art In Industry' exhibition of 1935, there appears to have been some practical problems, *Commercial Art* commenting:

Unfortunately the rooms were quite unsuitable in size, shape and decoration for a display of modern industrial art.

A model of a British European Airway's mobile exhibition stand, 1962 (designer, Andrew Radwan).

Museum put the Council of Industrial Design on the map, or the Council of Industrial Design showed Londoners where to find the Victoria & Albert Museum.

Apart from especially constructed pavilions and permanent buildings, mobile exhibitions became a necessity, particularly during WWII, when information and propaganda needed to reach across the country. Very few, even sizable, towns had halls large enough or with adequate access, for government exhibitions, even if they did have town halls. James Holland, writing on mobile exhibitions in Misha Black's book referred to most provincial town halls as having 'repellent interior aspects', inferring the need for them to be camouflaged to host any exhibitions the government held, if the desired effect was to be achieved.

A great variety of vehicles have been used for touring exhibitions, particularly in wartime and in the early post-war years, including trailers, lorries, buses, trains and ships. Trains became a particular favourite. As early as 1934, HMV had a show train exhibiting its latest products around the country and boasting that not only was it visited by thousands of commoners, but also by 10 Lord Mayors, 43 Mayors and 3 Baronets! Two post-war examples are the 1947 Atomic Scientists Association's 'Atomic Energy' exhibition designed by Peter Moro and Robin Day, and the 1949 Allied Iron Founders two fifty foot converted train coaches used to display the merchandise of some twenty two of its member companies. For

National Gallery; nor of Ashton's general disdain for exhibition designers, declaring he could do as well with the odd carpenter and electrician. Suffice it to say that BCMI was an arranged marriage, the CoID having considered other suitors beforehand! James Gardner recorded of how the plans for the exhibition shocked Ashton by reducing his 'dignified marble halls into theatre', and Gordon Russell, the Director of CoID wrote wryly of the whole shindig:

...in my more irresponsible moments I argued with [Ashton] as to whether the Victoria & Albert

Above: 'Atomic Energy' exhibition train, 1947.
Far right: Plan of Festival of Britain touring exhibition ship, 'Campania', 1951 (designer, James Holland).

this the outside of the coaches were dramatically clad in metal sheets with 'Ironfounders Exhibition Train' emblazoned in red letters; whilst the inside was sectioned into display spaces, a reception area, a twenty four seat cinema, and even a cocktail bar. Even the British Transport Commission resorted to adapted coaches when it decided a travelling exhibition would best suit its need to publicise its activities; one comment wished such facilities could be put in use for everyday travellers.

The most ambitious mobile exhibitions mounted in the 20th century were the two for the Festival of Britain. From the early planning days for the Festival it was intended that although the main sites would be in London, as far as possible, it should be a nation-wide event, and part of this aim was to devise 'mini-South Bank exhibitions' to tour the country by

sea and by road. The 'Campania', a decommissioned aircraft carrier, was kitted out for the trip by James Holland, a designer with a long interest in maritime matters:

I hurried to Goreloch, where Campania lay in deep water among the moth-balled reserve fleet, an uncompromising lump of grey and rusty steel but with a large hangar deck well-suited for the purpose.

Holland had the challenge of not only designing an exhibition but to display the exhibits in such a way as to withstand weather and wave conditions, as the ship had 'all the stability of a biscuit tin'; and then there was the additional problem of having to arrange accommodation for the navigating and catering crew accompanying the exhibition. To cheer up the outside the ship was painted white with bunting decorating the masts. In some five months Campania visited some ten cities and towns around the coast, staying from ten days to a fortnight at each, with each venue profiting as they would from the stay. Hull, for example, advertised that by visiting the ship people would also be able to see an Ellerman liner in from Australia, watch cargo vessels being unloaded, as well as view a good deal of the Humber coastline.

The Festival's 'Land Travelling' exhibition was claimed to be the biggest ever travelling exhibition at the time. Each of the towns visited – Manchester, Leeds, Birmingham and Nottingham, offered different sites and the exhibition layouts had to be adapted for each. The enormity of the project can be

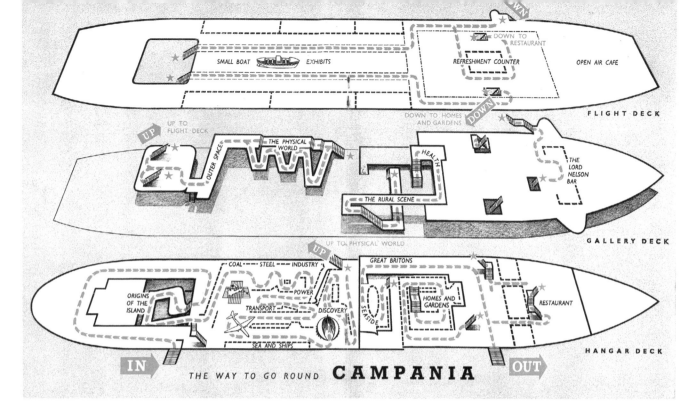

Small boat exhibits · Refreshment counter · Open air cafe · DOWN TO RESTAURANT · DOWN TO HOMES AND GARDENS · FLIGHT DECK · UP TO FLIGHT DECK · THE PHYSICAL WORLD · OUTER SPACE · HEALTH · THE LORD NELSON BAR · THE RURAL SCENE · GALLERY DECK · UP TO PHYSICAL WORLD · COAL · STEEL · INDUSTRY · GREAT BRITONS · POWER · ORIGINS OF THE ISLAND · TRANSPORT · DISCOVERY · HOMES AND GARDENS · RESTAURANT · SEASIDE · SEA AND SHIPS · HANGAR DECK · IN · OUT · THE WAY TO GO ROUND **CAMPANIA**

appreciated when some of the statistics are considered – 40,000 square feet in area, a steel façade of 120 by 50 feet, along with some 500 exhibits including a gas turbine – all of which travelled in lorries by road. A precise schedule of order of unloading, constructing, deconstructing and reloading was devised, with exact times for each activity.

Although mobile exhibitions continued to be used occasionally by companies and by government departments (as the Ministry of Labour for nursing recruitment and the Milk Marketing Board for general publicity, and designers, as James Gardner and Robin Day) sometimes interesting themselves in experimentation of adaptable travelling display units, the advantages of mobile exhibitions spreading the word were generally outweighed by their expense and physical limitations, and their use rapidly declined.

CELEBRATORY EXHIBITIONS

Few exhibitions were mounted with a single purpose; almost all, except perhaps some of the Ministry of Information wartime exhibitions had, underlying their being mounted, a concern for the economy. Some masked this by pretending, no, perhaps sincerely wishing, at the same time, to raise people's spirits encouraging feelings of optimism, and, to boost a feeling of pride in the nation's, or the Empire's achievements; for the latter that there existed such a grand bloc of countries, interdependent, and with common values, if not, overall, a common language.

The British Empire Exhibition, 1924–5

That people remember the British Empire Exhibition, if it is remembered much at all, is not so much for it having a key position in the history of exhibition design but, for railway enthusiasts, that it gave the first public viewing of 'The Flying Scotsman', and for philatelists, the Exhibition stamp being the first British 'commemorative' produced.

The idea of an exhibition extolling the British Empire, was mooted as early as 1913 by Lord Strathcona, who had been Vice-President of the 1908 Franco-British Exhibition and had been impressed by its impact. All ideas of an Empire Exhibition were halted by the onset of WWI, but not long after the Armistice, plans were revisited, and a large exhibition committee set up, representing as many interested parties as possible; a site was purchased; architects, builders and administrators appointed; and the deadline set (very soon found to be too ambitious) to coincide with the 1923 Football Cup Final, which, it was decided, should be played on the site.

An Exhibition Guide proclaimed the overall aim of mounting such a show:

The fundamental purpose of the British Empire Exhibition is serious. It is to stimulate trade, to

strengthen the bonds that bind the Mother Country to her Sister States and Daughter Nations, to bring all into a closer touch the one with the other; to enable all who own an allegiance to the British flag to meet on common ground, and to learn to know each other. It is a Family Party, to which every part of the Empire is invited and at which every part of the Empire is represented.

The British Empire Exhibition seems to have attracted more superlatives than any other, even than the Great Exhibition. It was described as the biggest, the grandest, show ever mounted – 15 miles of road, a 216 acre site, using 15,000,000 tons of concrete, with lakes holding 2,500,000 gallons of water, and more of the same. It was declared that 'Rome's immortal Coliseum would be lost within the stadium'. Knight and Sabey, in their book on the Exhibition, make no attempt to hold back their enthusiasm with intensely purple prose:

...the visitors had spread before them the wondrous reality of the British Empire, the might and magnitude – her grandeur and her glory ... the scene was without parallel in the history of mankind.

In design terms it was indeed something of a landmark. *Commercial Art* devoted many of its pages to it, the Editor writing:

Commercial Art takes a very serious interest in the British Empire Exhibition because it is the first important exhibition in this country in which the need for artistic arrangement has been fully realised.

The raising of exhibition aesthetics by this Exhibition started with its architecture. The architects appointed for the overall look of the site were Sir John W. Simpson and Maxwell Ayrton, each also involved in designing some of the buildings – Ayrton the British Government Pavilion, and the pair cooperating on the main Palaces. To ensure some harmony and uniformity of standards exhibitors were given a list of recommended architects. Sir Lawrence Weaver, who was given responsibility for ensuring the standard for the display of exhibits in the British Pavilion, was said to have 'combed the Continent for ideas which will make visitors want to see more, while getting less tired'. The displays of other countries were not in such safe hands, often given to government administrators, and, sometimes, even to their wives. The list of those making contributions to the pavilions of the colonies and dominions was splattered with Lords and Ladies and Sirs, as Lady Guggisberg, the wife of the Governor of the Gold Coast.

Uniformity was also achieved by the main buildings being constructed with ferro-concrete, with steel frameworks. Concrete was relatively cheap and quick to handle, and the Exhibition site rapidly grew as 'a city of concrete' – even down to the Exhibition

Kennedy North's 1923 map of the grounds of the British Empire Exhibition, Wembley Park.

lions and its lamp posts. The Press applauded with such comments as:

It is well to insist that here we have no ephemeral structure designed to endure for a season and to pass thereafter into desolation and decay. And: ...a place which makes an architect proud of his profession.

In the course of time, inevitably, much 'desolation' did take place, with most of the Empire Pavilions being pulled down or converted into factories and offices, the Stadium being the most long lasting structure.

Introducing an altogether lighter note to the site than the solid pavilions, were the colourful, playful kiosks, designed by Joseph Emberton – some forty small structures, alongside the lake and down the main avenue. Cynically these were possibly introduced to allow a number of companies to advertise (advertising being largely excluded from the pavilions), and also to increase incomings, as the kioks were rented out. Emberton was considered 'a young architect with his own ideas'. Weaver at first commissioned him, and his then partner, Percy Westwood, to design both buildings and display stands but Emberton is sometimes recorded as designing the kiosks with Westwood, sometimes by himself – whichever, he was to have a hectic six

months working on them. He made use of each company's established advertising and packaging, and described the result as 'posters in three-dimensions'. The results nowadays might be described as 'whacky' – Sharp's Creamy Toffee kiosk a structure of modelled toffee tins, the various railway companies as mini-railway stations, and so on. Rosemary Inde, Emberton's biographer, described his idiosyncratic approach:

...the last echoes of Successionalism together with the result of Emberton's time in Egypt ... small, white and severly sculptural and with ... an appropriate Imperial flavour ... most are slightly battered in outline and have a joggled parapet, with a flat roof, a dome or a barrel vault, and either an inset or jutting balcony.

Commercial Art ignored the idiosyncracies, considering the kiosks justifiable both from an aesthetic and from a commercial viewpoint. The British Empire Exhibition can claim to be the first British exhibition to have an emblem to represent it. Just as Abram Games' head of Britannia came to stand for anything to do with the Festival of Britain, so did the Baynard Press's F.C. Herrick's 'Lion' come to symbolize the Empire and its Exhibition. The design must have been accepted fairly early on in the planning as *Commercial Art* was writing about it in 1923:

From its pedestal on poster and booklet it regards with patient confidence the preparation for the exhibition over which it will preside.

Left: 'The man who wouldn't go to Wembley', *Punch* cartoon. **Above:** Sharp's Toffee Kiosk, Wembley (designers, Westwood and Emberton).

There was, inevitably, a certain amount of controversy before the Lion was actually accepted, but eventually it was agreed that such a creature embodied what was considered such qualities as appropriately representing the Empire as power, prestige, dignity, vigilance, etc. Herrick's Lion appeared everywhere – from flag to poster to leaflet – and the lion theme was also used for six large concrete lions to stand in front of the British Government Pavilion as well as appearing on the exhibition medal, designed by Percy Metcalfe. *Commercial Art* declared it a success:

Mr. Herrick's Lion, clear-cut, alive, is a triumph even when it is reduced to postage stamp size and even reproduced at the bottom of advertisements.

But, perhaps the greatest indication that the Lion had been accepted by the nation was when it featured in a Punch cartoon entitled 'The Man who would not go to Wembley' in which the said man, in bed, is having nightmares of an endless line of lions chasing him.

The Exhibition produced vast quantities of printed matter – official guides, handbooks and catalogues, daily programmes, posters and postcards. Information was sent out prior to the Exhibition, and afterwards. There was said to have been five and a half million information folders alone, designed by Kennedy North, posted out to the colonies and dominions in advance; and the Department of Trade and Industry placed over four hundred advertisements in overseas newspapers and magazines.

F.C. Herrick's alphabet inspired by the Trajan column.

Lots of material had blank spaces for countries, and other exhibitors, to fill in as they would. *Commercial Art* found much of this output 'lacking in vision' and 'rather humdrum'. It was particularly scathing of the posters:

The shop is open, the merchandise is there to be seen and bought, but the window has not yet been properly dressed ... The lack of imagination can be seen in the posters; all of them more or less naturalistic representations of the exhibition and a few fireworks.

An estimate of the vast numbers of posters produced was 100,000 Double Crown and 450,000 Double Royal, largely showing views of the Exhibition as Frank Newbold's 'Tour the Empire at Wembley' or Fred Taylor's enormous poster, some 40ft long and 10ft high; and even when the site was not being illustrated there was much use made of the flags of the dominions, of famous Empire personalities, scenes of Empire produce, and other fairly traditional images. And scenes of the Empire and the Exhibition site were largely the subject matter of the hundreds of postcards on sale, the official photographer being Cambell Gray; Raphael Tuck alone printed 48 views of the Queen's Doll House which was an Exhibition exhibit. For the mania of exhibition ephemera collecting the British Empire Exhibition is a gold mine. And then there was the Exhibition stamp, selected by a committee of worthies from a short-list of six, including Herrick, the wood-engraver Noel Rooke and Eric Gill (just

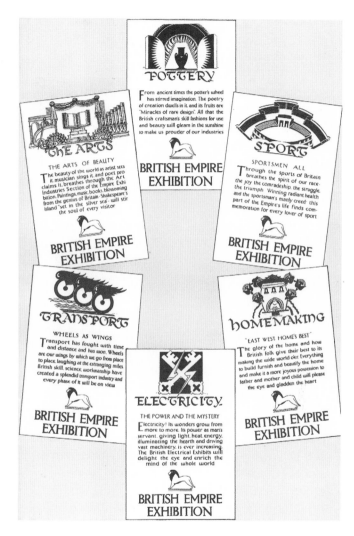

Edward McKnight Kauffer's posters for the Exhibition.

considered as a reserve). It was Gill and another reserve, Harold Nelson who were chosen, and it was estimated that on the first day, by 4pm a million stamps had been sold.

Perhaps the most notable advance in exhibition design at the British Empire Exhibition was in the exhibition signing. Weaver, who was concerned to bring some harmony into its design, commissioned Herrick to produce a new alphabet. This produced a certain amount of scoffing from the press – 'Trajan, Trajan, all the way' – as Herrick had based his design on lettering on Trajan's Column. The alphabet was adopted not only for the signposts but throughout the site, which was admired for the unity it brought, but, by some, considered too small to be legible – the whole point of a sign!

As to the actual displays – for the main Palaces and the British Government Pavilion some uniformity was achieved by working through trade associations, each with a single architect, rather than having individual companies and organisations resort to their own idiosyncratic styles; but little is recorded about individual stands. In retrospect the Exhibition can be rated as significant in design terms in that there was considerable central overall design control, in that it was experimental with materials, in that it was one of the first to make extensive use of electricity in its working models and information displays, and in that it used professional architects and designers. Yet in other ways it tended toward traditional practice. Gossop,

the most important artists' agent of the time, and himself a designer, considered it overall 'too correct and proper', and 'very much on its best behaviour'; *Commercial Art* found the graphics 'staid'; and, even one of the handbooks referred to the British exhibits as being 'displayed in the quiet unobtrusive and impersonal fashion that one associates with Whitehall'!

The Empire Exhibition, Scotland, 1938

An Empire Exhibition in as architecturally backward country as Britain cannot expect to draw on the same richness of architectural talent as an international exhibition. Architecture Review

Scotland had mounted major exhibitions in 1888 and 1901, and a group of Scottish businessmen, led by Sir Cecil Weir, decided to use the 50th anniversary of the first of these to boost the Scottish economy so badly hit by the depression of the 1930s.

The handbook to the Exhibition initially suggests that the Empire is the reason for the exhibition – to show the resources and potentialities of the Empire to a new generation and to foster British trade – but then comes a more blatant Scottish motive:

To stimulate work and production and to direct attention to Scotland's historical and scenic attractions.

The characteristics of this particular exhibition were not only that it celebrated things Scottish, that it was designed by professionals, that although it was concerned with trade it also concerned itself

with public service, that it was 'modernist', but, for the first time for any kind of British exhibition, it involved named women architects and designers, probably more so even than the Festival of Britain.

The eminence gris, imbuing the whole site with his modernist vision was Thomas Tait, the most celebrated Scottish architect of the time. He headed up a team of some nine architects, the best known of whom were Basil Spence and Jack Coia, both brought up in Scotland and both training there, Spence at the Edinburgh School of Art and Coia at the Glasgow School of Architecture.

The site for the Exhibition, Bellahouston Park, presented Tait with the challenge of designing an exhibition around a hill. Rather than side-step the problem, Tait was to make a feature of it, mounting it

Previous spread: Tait's Tower, Empire Exhibition, Glasgow, 1938. **Left:** Construction of the Palace of Industry North. **Opposite left:** 20ft model steel furnace, United Kingdom Pavilion. **Opposite right:** ICI Pavilion.

what became a major attraction – a pavilion for ICI. Its three towers, symbolizing Earth, Air and Water, were illuminated by a beam of light representing Fire. The whole effect was conceived to demonstrate ICI's developing interest in synthetic materials and non-ferrous metals, with such contemporary products as Perspex being shown off under a glass rotunda.

The commissioned women architects and designers, as the men, were all Scottish or had trained in Scotland. Margaret Brodie, born and brought up in Glasgow, one of the first women to qualify as an architect in Scotland, worked in Burnet, Tait and Lorne's London office. Brodie not only designed the Exhibition's 15,000 sq. ft. 'Women of the Empire' Pavilion, but acted as site supervisor, overseeing the construction from a small wooden hut onsite. She is recorded as seeing it as 'having the time of my life'. She was barely thirty when the Exhibition was in its planning stage. A number of other women contributed to the Exhibition, mainly for Brodie's Pavilion, including Lady Kennet (who had been married to Captain Scott) and Phyllis Bone (who had trained at the Edinburgh College of Art), both sculptresses, and Phoebe Stabler, a ceramicist.

Although not a matter of direct interest in relation to exhibition design, the Empire Exhibition,

with his Tower of the Empire, and having the slopes adorned with giant staircases and cascades of water.

There was said to be over one hundred pavilions, with much of the architecture a stream-lined modernism, making use of a considerable amount of pre-fabrication – steel and timber frames with panels of cement. Coia designed the Roman Catholic Pavilion, one of five denominational buildings. Spence had three commissions – the North and South Scottish Pavilions (resonating in blue paint, with flat roofs, their silhouettes described as 'straight, strict and formal') and the Council of Art and Industry's ideal Scottish house. He also designed

Scotland, had a considerable number of buildings, and displays within buildings, devoted to public service activities. In addition to the denominational ones, other organisations showing included the Corporation of Glasgow, the Home Office (for health and safety at work), the Ministry of Labour (with an actual employment exchange), the League of Nations (with a Peace Pavilion), and all three Services (the Army, the RAF, and the Royal Navy).

Quite the reverse of the *Architectural Review's* doom-ridden prediction of unprogressive architecture, the Exhibition proved something of an architectural triumph, showing off not only the British, or rather the Scottish, acceptance of European design trends, but demonstrating the use of new materials and methods of construction. John Summerson, the architectural historian, wrote not only of its success, but of the renewed morale it brought:

...a major achievement of the exhibition was not just that it had demonstrated modern architecture to Scotland, but that it was dynamic, producing an architecture that was exciting and fun, and not purely cerebral, that it gave Scotland an air of quality and chic providing an important step on the road to recovery.

The poignancy that it was an exhibition about an empire that was crumbling, that it was preaching peace only some nine months before the start of WWII, that the site itself was swept clean with no 'modernism', or indeed anything else, remaining apart from the Palace of Arts, does not take away from it its good intentions, its architectural courage, and the opportunity it gave to so many young architects and designers to test their talents.

The Festival of Britain, 1951

I was stirred and rather moved by the gallant inventiveness of what I saw on the South Bank ... I had a vision of a whole gang of youngish untidy enthusiasts who refused to be daunted by vast programmes and lack of space, shortage of materials and sullen weather, but planned and sketched with zest, gaily invented, and defied, on our behalf, as well as theirs, the foul fiends of dullness, defeat and pessimism.
J.B. Priestley

It did put a moment of dreamworld into a lot of people's lives.
James Gardner

The literature issuing from, and, in retrospect, on, the Festival of Britain can fill library shelves. To the two major books covering the Festival – *A Tonic to the Nation* (1976) and *The Autobiography of a Nation* (2003), can be added a third, with a comprehensive coverage – *The Festival of Britain, a land and its people* (2012) – what more is there to add? And yet, in a book on exhibitions, and in a section on celebratory ones, the Festival cannot be omitted in that it was the first, and possibly the last, in several aspects.

Previous spread: Aerial view of the Festival of Britain South Bank site, 1951. Above: A Festival signpost at the South Bank (designers, Milner Gray and Robin Day), with Skylon in background. Right: The Skylon at night.

It was the first British exhibition aiming to be 'nationwide' – Britain was to be celebrated by as many British people as possible. The main Festival sites were, in London – on the South Bank, at Battersea and in the Science Museum – with a major exhibition in Glasgow and a smaller one in Belfast, along with two touring exhibitions – on land and by sea. In addition, Gerald Barry, the Festival's Director General, encouraged organisations to arrange exhibitions across the country on their own special interests including the Council of Industrial Design, the Churches, and the like; the National Book League, alone, was responsible for some eighty or so such exhibitions. When it is added to all this activity the various projects put on by local authorities, from villages to metropolitan areas, there was little of Great Britain that didn't exhibit itself in 1951!

When the South Bank site alone is considered, it provided a number of original exhibition features, and, if not firsts, then at least most developed to a significant scale. The idea of exhibitions telling a story had already been used by the Ministry of Information during the war, and, at the Festival, the narrative of 'The Land and the People' virtually determined the show. Barry, with his newspaper background, along with some of his journalist buddies as his caption writers, at hand, sketched out the overall story line with which the 'visual' people – the architects and designers – had to run. Hugh Casson, the Festival's Director of Architecture, recorded that they worked with 'the script in one hand and a map

principle of the picturesque in which the future of town planning as a visual art assuredly lies.

A further character of the Festival was its extensive use of sculpture and art, partly to enhance the architecture and displays, but also to give the whole site cultural brownie points. Besides the various pieces of sculpture, mainly representing the human form, by such major artists as Henry Moore, Lynn Chadwick, Reg Butler, and Barbara Hepworth, more use was made of murals, probably more than at any other exhibition to that date. As this is a neglected aspect of exhibition design generally, a later chapter is included touching on the subject.

The effectiveness, the validation of an exhibition, needs to be related to its aims, and, in the instance of the Festival, there appear to have been a number of different agendas. The original nub of an idea for a festival in 1951 had merely been to celebrate the centenary of the Great Exhibition. Barry's declared statement of intent was that the Festival would show:

The British contribution to civilization past, present and future in the arts, in science and technology and in industrial design.

Much was written about needing some kind of affirmation that we were a united kingdom, a phoenix literally arising from the ashes (from the bombings) and with the energy to rebuild. Herbert Morrison, on behalf of the government, emphasized the morale boosting aspect of the planned Festival, with his:

...we ought to do something jolly ... we need something to give Britain a lift...

of the site in the other'. The narrative was so key to the exhibition planners that visitors were advised to use the assigned circulation route so that the story could be unfolded in a systematic way; Dylan Thomas commented, wryly, that 'it was likely to lead people into the Thames'.

Another original aspect was that the actual layout of the South Bank was, in itself, to be an example of how future town planning might develop – how structure and landscaping might be balanced to provide decent environments for future populations. The *Architectural Review* considered that it:

...represents that realization in urban terms of the

Similarly Harold Nicolson wrote that a reason for the Festival was:

...to dissipate the gloom that hung like a pea-soup above the heads of the generation of 1951.

And then there was the possible political motive, that some, the more conservative elements, accused the government of using the Festival not only to 'lift people's hearts' after the suffering, the restrictions, the drabness of the war years, but to validate and gain support for the government's planned development of a welfare state.

Of course the architects and designers had their own agendas, so many of them young, only in their 20s and 30s, eager to prove themselves, to gain reputations upon which they could build after the Festival high jinx had ended; a few even had the idealistic aims to introduce progressive designs and to educate the public to good design.

Well, against the criterion of 'something jolly' the Festival can certainly be rated a success. Arnold Wesker came away from it 'feeling you could dance just like Kelly'; whilst Hugh Casson, himself, wrote of the joy of 'dancing in the rain'; *Display* rated it 'fun, but fun with a purpose'; and whether it was the visitors, or most of those involved in the Festival's mounting 'fun' was a word very frequently used. Even working against tight deadlines and bad weather was rated 'fun'; Paul Wright, the Festival's Director of Public Relations wrote of the pleasure his staff got from being involved, which, he thought, well-compensated them for 'late hours and tired eyes'. In *A Tonic for the Nation* space was given for both participants, and visitors, memories, and in spite of restrictions, strikes, bad weather, these accounts are peppered with such words as 'uplifting', 'jubilant', 'magic', 'exciting', 'a shot-in-the-arm'. Nicolson, in the *Spectator*, wrote a typical response:

...in place of the cemetery I had dreaded I found a maternity home, gay with pink and blue and resonant with cries and gurgles of the world that is to be. I returned to the drab outside encouraged and entranced.

Against the criteria of 'furthering careers' the Festival can also be rated a success. To take Hugh Casson as an example, not only was he knighted for his Festival labours, but, having largely been previously known for his architectural writings, he now found numerous design doors opening to him. His wife wrote – 'He is quite a famous little man now. You can hardly open a paper without seeing something about him'. Willy de Majo, the chief designer for the Ulster exhibition, recorded that it had helped him be recognized as being more than a package and display man, but a fully-fledged exhibition designer. And it certainly furthered the future of the Council of Industrial Design for their photographic record of some 10,000 or so products needed for the Festival provided the basis of its permanent index, which became its main raison d'etre for the establishment of the Design Centre.

There definitely was a Festival Spirit but was there a Festival 'Style', and how far did the Festival

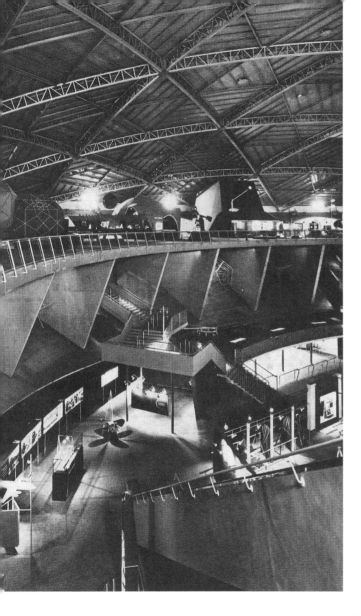

contribute to the advancement of design? As a young student from a two-up-two-down terraced house in the North of England, exposed to the visual wonders of the Festival, most of the pundits on this matter read sourly to me. The majority suggest that at least for the cognoscenti, the elite educated in continental modernism, the Festival, as far as design is concerned, was 'old hat'. Rayner Banham wrote with an arrogant kind of glee that the Festival architecture was derived from the Italians, that its layout came from Corbusier, that Ernest Race was merely rehashing Charles Eames, that:

...there was nothing very new about what could be seen at the Festival – though the British deserved a bit of a pat on the back for having finally caught up.

And worse – that they had 'finally caught up with a package that was already exhausted'. In Banham's view – 'influence-wise the Festival died a-borning'. And when Banham's view appears to have been supported by such a guru as the experienced exhibition designer Misha Black that:

The Festival spotlit and gently pushed forward an already existing style – it did not create one.

One is nearly convinced by Banham's argument that the Festival style was a myth carried forward by interested parties, as the architectural press and the Council of Industrial Design. Charles Plouviez, described as merely a humble employee at the

41

Festival, perhaps wrote one of the most damning assessments:

As an exhibition the South Bank was a failure. The thematic treatment fought with the exhibits and the whole was too indigestible for the visitor to absorb. And the exhibition itself as a communication technique was already on the way out, displaced by better colour-printing, easier travel – and above all – TV.

Yet a few lone voices pointed to the facts that, until the Festival, London had hardly any 'modernist'

Below left: *Black Eyes & Lemonade* exhibition catalogue (designer, Barbara Jones), Whitechapel Art Gallery, London. **Below:** Sea and Ships Pavilion (architect, Basil Spence), South Bank. **Right:** Entrance hall, Exhibition of Industrial Power, Glasgow. **Far right:** Spiral casing positioned for display at the Industrial Power exhibit.

architecture, that the layout, landscaping and treatment of the Festival spaces directly affected municipal planning and redevelopment, and that the Festival's use of molecular patterning not only found

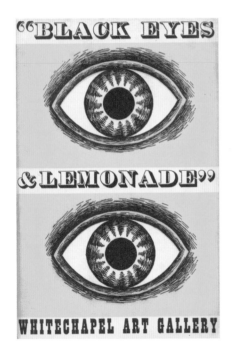

its way into 'coffee bars and renovated pubs', but into furniture and carpeting and textiles, dressing ordinary people's homes. The Festival may not have been sufficiently progressive, in design terms, for the cultured elite, but for the general population it was an eye-opener, having them rushing off to Heals and Dunn's of Bromley, and out-of-London equivalents, with colourful Lucienne Day and spikey Ernest Race lookalikes replacing 1930s fawns and solid wood. Although the political message carried by the Festival – that Britain was not only recovering, but that a fairer and more decent society was on its way – may have begun to falter with the defeat of the Labour

Party in the 1951 election, the stimulus the Festival provided for young architects and designers and the young soon-to-be home owners to *think* 'good design' was to permeate the '50s into the swinging '60s. It may have been sniffily dismissed as passé by its critics, but the Festival of Britain had more influence on the way ordinary people felt and lived than any exhibition before, or for that matter, since.

TRADE EXHIBITIONS

The British Industries Fairs

...the BIF is not merely a national or an imperial institution but a medium for the promotion of international trade.

Few people, nowadays, apart from a small band interested in exhibition history, remember the British Industries Fairs. Yet these were immense affairs, claimed by some to be the largest national trade fairs in the world. They were government sponsored, run annually from 1915 to 1954, on sites adding up to nearly a million square feet, and, from a design viewpoint, reported upon critically in the relevant press, in particular *Commercial Art/Art & Industry* and *Display*; and, at least in the post-WWII years, attracting some of the major exhibition designers in the country. For example, in the 1947 BIF, James Gardner had real paraquets on the Harella stand, Hulme Chadwick presented a stand for the Leather, Footwear and Allied Industries that was considered 'boldly conceived', Basil Spence and Robin Day designed a stand for ICI, 'almost overwhelming in scope', Christopher Nicholson and Robert Goodden constructed a 'sensational' stand for Tube Investments, Robert Goodden and Richard Guyatt were responsible for providing 'two brilliant stands' for the Council of Industrial Design explaining the development of a design and the function of a design centre, de Majo designed one of his striking stands for Miles Martin Pen Co., whilst Milner Gray provided a more modest one for Goray Skirts – they were all there.

In his book on exhibition design Misha Black wrote that Great Britain needed the dynamite of a world war before they established a contemporary national trade exhibition. It was early in WWI that the government, concerned as to how the war might affect overseas trade, established what was

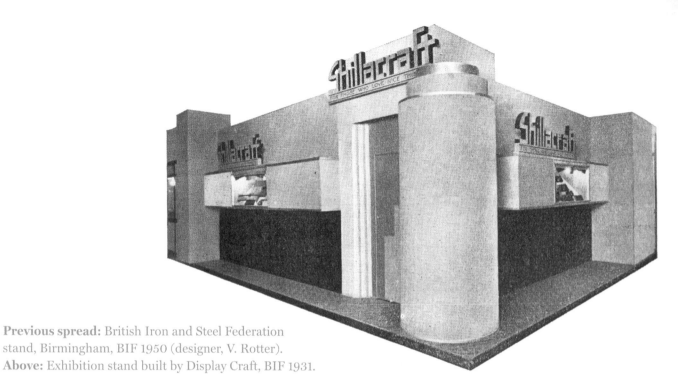

Previous spread: British Iron and Steel Federation stand, Birmingham, BIF 1950 (designer, V. Rotter). **Above:** Exhibition stand built by Display Craft, BIF 1931.

to become the Commercial Relations and Export Department of the Board of Trade; and it was this that was to have responsibility for running the BIF on its London sites, whilst the Birmingham Chamber of Commerce ran that part of the Fairs which were on the Castle Bromwich site.

Originally the Fairs were mounted at the White City and Olympia sites in London for textiles and 'light products', whilst building and the heavy industries were displayed at Castle Bromwich. Although some records state that the switch from the White City to Earls Court occurred in 1929, the design press was still recording stands at the former into the mid-1930s. This seems more likely as the Earls Court venue was not refurbished until 1935, and Knight, the historian of the White City, has it as definitive that the switch to Earls Court occurred in 1938. As Castle Bromwich was not built until 1920, the Fairs to that date were just held at White City and Olympia.

As with so many other exhibitions, both annual and one-off, there was the perennial problem for the

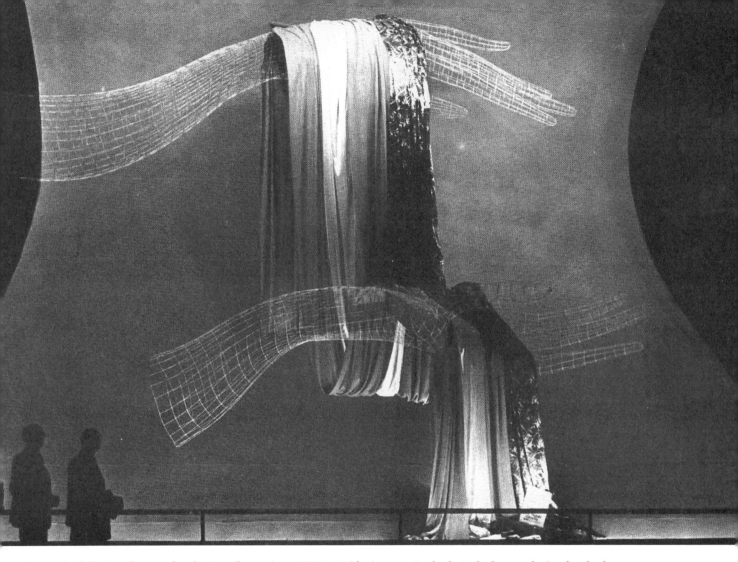

Central exhibition feature for the Textile section, BIF 1947 (designers, Cockade Ltd., from a design by the late Christopher Nicholson).

and control of standard features had not curbed the imagination of the exhibition'. Yet by 1950 *Display* had begun to feel the pendulum had swung too far, that although 'standardisation controls vulgarity' it can produce mediocrity. The new broom Council of Industrial Design, in its journal *Design*, spelt out the compromise emerging at BIF – with the minnows standardized and the big guns given free rein:

The outstanding success of the 1949 BIF in London, from the point of view of imaginative exhibition technique were those free-standing

BIF as to how much overall control of design there should be. *Display* in the 1930s complained of the frequent muddle at Olympia of the 'shrieking discord of colour' and continually argued for the 'conception of the exhibition to be "one vast impressive display".' Looking back to the interwar BIF one curiously worded comment, presumably referring to some of the more technical displays, was:

At one time these exhibitions lacked plan and cohesion and seemed to offer little more than intellectual food for questing schoolboys.

Uniformity came to the fore for the 1947 and 1948 BIF, when Basil Spence was appointed overall designer, and it was reported that 'standard shells

non-conformist displays that did not observe the standard fascia, colour and lettering to which their smaller neighbours were subject.

ICI was one of the 'big guns' showing at the BIF. *Display* commented upon how the post-war style of exhibition design, particularly post-Festival of Britain, suited ICI products:

...few products lend themselves to contemporary presentation as well as chemicals; abstract and symbolic shapes, a feature of modern exhibition

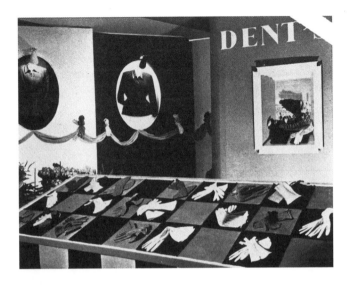

design, are in sympathy with merchandise itself recognizable by formulae and equation.

It was not only the match that led to ICI's impressive post-war displays, but the fact that they were employing the best designers of the time – Basil Spence, Robin Day, and V. Rotter. Spence & Day had produced their stand for the 1947 Fair – 'imaginative in conception and lavish in execution', and Day designed a further one for ICI Metals in 1953. It was Hulme Chadwick that ICI was to use for displaying its new products – Ardil and Terylene – each at different stages of development and neither yet being produced in quantity; yet ICI had taken a main stand and needed a 'showing off' display. A rare detailed account of the challenge of designing an exhibition stand, in this instance by Chadwick, was given in *Display*. With little lead time and new techniques to handle, the manufacturing side needed to be cajoled to produce as much material as they could, whilst some of the leading designers in haute couture, and in furniture, including John Cavenagh, Digby Morton and Ernest Race, needed to be persuaded to develop their designs taking into account what material was likely to be available. In addition to planning settings for clothes and furniture, Chadwick set out to tell the story of each new product, from their respective starts – from

Left: Poster for BIF, London & Birmingham, 1932 (designer, Tom Purvis). **Above:** Stand for Ministry of Labour by G.W. Pollard (with features by Hugh Casson and Richard Guyatt), 1948.

groundnuts and oil – to the finished fibres to be used variously in fishing nets and gossamer fabrics. Chadwick, a hardened exhibition designer, provided the required wow factor – pylons draped with the materials, shop-windows for the clothes, a director's office for business deals and large amounts of information:

The whole exhibition [ICI] was a remarkable example of the results that can be achieved when industry and design work hand-in-hand, when each party gives the other help and encouragement and both parties clearly see a vision of something new.

As an addendum it is worth noting the posters advertising BIF, in particular the ones by Tom Purvis in the 1930s. C.G. Holme, writing of these in *Commercial Art* in 1934 told of Purvis catching the spirit of the Fairs:

Throughout the many committee meetings which I am certain must have taken place, and amongst the conflicting opinions of what was or was not required of these posters, there evolved a certain line of thought which the artist was quick to grasp.

The theme settled upon was variations of Britannia, but Purvis produced not a hackneyed Britannia sitting on her throne, but a very 'macho' one, in strident red, white and dark blue, holding an enlarged trident and with bent finger commanding

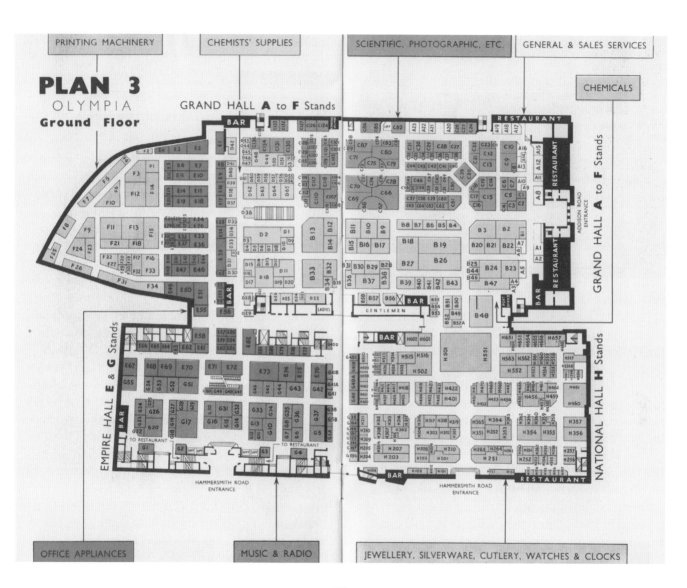

PLAN 3
OLYMPIA
Ground Floor

GRAND HALL **A** to **F** Stands

PRINTING MACHINERY

CHEMISTS' SUPPLIES

SCIENTIFIC, PHOTOGRAPHIC, ETC.

GENERAL & SALES SERVICES

CHEMICALS

RESTAURANT

GRAND HALL **A** to **F** Stands

ADDISON ROAD ENTRANCE

EMPIRE HALL **E** & **G** Stands

NATIONAL HALL **H** Stands

HAMMERSMITH ROAD ENTRANCE

HAMMERSMITH ROAD ENTRANCE

TO RESTAURANT

TO RESTAURANT

OFFICE APPLIANCES

MUSIC & RADIO

JEWELLERY, SILVERWARE, CUTLERY, WATCHES & CLOCKS

Book of designs entered in the 'Daily Mail Architects Competition for Labour-Saving Bungalows', 1922.

the visitors' attendance. Purvis was to produce posters for BIF for over ten years. None of the BIF posters, either before or after, quite symbolized the Fair's intent so well, albeit McKnight Kauffer produced several for London Transport, announcing the Fair's arrival, both in the 1920s and '30s.

The BIF was run every year with the exception of 1925 (presumably because of a possible clash with the British Empire Exhibition) and the war period. Although some of the most brilliant designing took place after WWII, into the early 1950s, the Fairs began to run into debt, and the government eventually decided that it would be more economic for

manufacturers to take their goods directly to their clients, at home and overseas, rather than expect the customers to travel annually to London.

The Daily Mail 'Ideal Home Exhibition'

The Daily Mail 'Ideal Home Exhibition' ran for nearly one hundred years, from its inauguration in 1908 until the Daily Mail sold it in 2009.

When it came to exhibition design it was something of a Cinderella, at least until after WWII, and even then it tended to be overshadowed by the other annual shindig – the British Industries Fair. Commentary on the Ideal Home Exhibition has tended to be from the viewpoint of the social, rather than the design historian on its reflection on how technological, political, economic and social changes influenced consumer choice and aspirations.

Generally the design press gave it scant notice. Weaver in his mammoth tome on exhibition design in 1925 gives it only one mention. *Commercial Art* and *Art & Industry*, prior to WWII, allotted it only one article, in 1931, and that by Douglas Tanner, described as the architect of the exhibition at the time. It was not until the late 1940s that the exhibition was taken at all seriously in design terms, when such designers as Beverley Pick and Misha Black were to be involved. And it was not until the 1990s that Deborah Ryan, in her comprehensively researched book, actually makes reference to the 'look' of the Exhibition and records the names of several of its

Draft design of the Daily Mail Ideal Home Exhibition at Olympia, 1931 (architect, Douglas G. Tanner).

architects (along with those architects who were actually having their planned houses on show).

The V&A, which holds the Exhibition's archives in its index, states, curiously, and maintaining the social historian's viewpoint:

Lord Northcliffe, proprietor of the Daily Mail, founded the Ideal Home Exhibition in 1908 at London's Olympia Exhibition Centre, in the spirit of social reform, to stimulate debate about better housing conditions.

Nothing could be further from the truth! Northcliffe not only found the project unwelcome, but refused to visit it in its first few years and declared that 'The Daily Mail does not need these

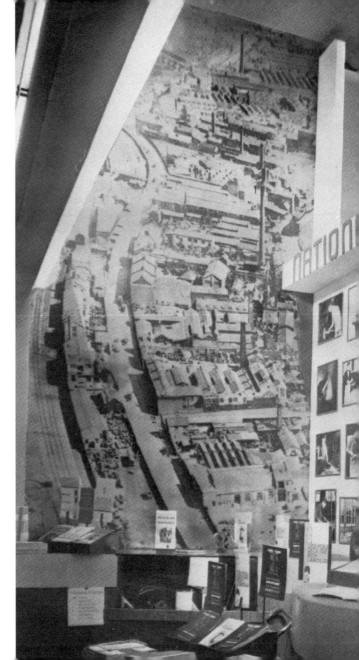

artificial supports'. From the start the Ideal Home Exhibition was an advertising stunt, with little, if any, concern for 'better housing conditions' or any other social issues for that matter. It was known, within the newspaper, as 'Wareham's little sideline'. In fact it was the brainchild of Wareham Smith, and his protégé Frederick Bussy, working in the small, at that time insignificant, advertising office of the newspaper, at the start of the 20th century. Wareham Smith's intentions were empire building rather than social reforming when he sent Bussy out on the road to attract more advertising. Smith described Bussy:

He was a genius. He was full of ideas, but, like geniuses he needed keeping down to earth. I had to sit on him pretty hard continually.

Despite Smith's continual need to rein Bussy in, together they hatched up the idea for an Ideal Home Exhibition. Bussy, on his sales trips, began to appreciate that there were myriads of companies, related to the building industry, ripe for plucking as potential advertisers, which previously had tended only to have contact with buyers via architects. The pair decided to take Olympia for the purpose of holding an Ideal Home Exhibition to encourage a more direct contact between the building industry and the general public, that could later be maintained by advertisements placed in the paper; the Lord Mayor opened the Exhibition with nothing but praise for the worthy Daily Mail! It was only gradually that the Daily Mail began to appreciate the kudos of linking the exhibition with social concerns and good causes.

Where design was mentioned in relation to the Ideal Home Exhibitions it was mainly concerned with the products and the houses on show, and not on the actual layout of the Exhibition or the design of the show stands. It is only with Douglas Tanner's article in *Commercial Art* that one gains any appreciation of the 'designing' of the Exhibtion itself. As Architect of the Exhibition in 1931 he wrote of his concern:

...that the exhibition should in itself form an interesting design and not merely give the impression of a conglomeration of highly coloured stands of all shapes and sizes.

In spite of the 'hue and cry' from some of the exhibitors, the Daily Mail organizer, a Mr. Gordon, decided to back Tanner's radical plan towards unified design in a small part of the Exhibition, with stands of standard size and shape. As this was judged a success, more and more of the Exhibition became standardized in subsequent years so that, as Tanner had intended, the stand would show off the merchandise and not overshadow it. *Display*, in 1934, approved such standardization:

The shimmering walls of steel and the regularity of the stand design struck a definitely harmonious

FITTER
BRITAIN
PROGRAMME

NATIONAL FITNESS COUNCIL
IDEAL HOME EXHIBITION

OLYMPIA, 1938

*note and, relieved by the foil of blue gauze that
screened-in the roof, the picture was impressive...*

It was Tanner who, in addition, began to open
out the stands and deny exhibitors their preferred
'columns, fascias and roofing'. Nevertheless Tanner
realized that the show needed a central eye-catcher,
and he allowed extravagant free rein design for the
Main Hall.

*The velarium in the Main Hall consisted of
14,000 yards of material, with roughly 15 miles of*
*stitching. The canvas on the end sheet was 170 feet
long and 70 feet high and is believed to be the largest
scenic canvas ever produced.*

Although the architects of the show houses were
usually named it was not really until after WWII
that exhibition architects and display designers
for the Ideal Home Exhibition were individually
acknowledged to any extent. *Display* claimed the
first post-war Exhibition – 'a displaymen's own show'
in spite of the problems of mounting a show in such

Far left: Central Hall, 1951 exhibition (designer, James Gardner). **Above left:** Construction workers prepare for an exhibition. **Above right:** Manchester Oil Refinery Group stand (designer, James Gardner; mural, Robert Scanlan).

conditions. The press expressed the challenge:

Seldom can an exhibition have been projected under less favourable conditions. Seldom has an exhibition architect conjured such an auspicious show from so little.

From the Daily Mail end Stuart Maclean was to have responsibility in the post-war years and James Gardner became involved with the design. Gardner provided a number of stands for Newnes, the publisher, and the Design Research Unit was named for a stand for the Ministry of Town and Country Planning. Beverley Pick wrote that in spite of it being a period of austerity the design of the Exhibition was becoming increasingly professional:

...it has demonstrated a new high level of stand and display design, on the whole, far above anything seen before the war.

And 'professional' it had become; in addition to Gardner and the DRU (in particular Misha Black, Robert Gutmann and Austin Frazer), Christopher Nicholson and V. Rotter were also commissioned, with Stephen Tallents' 'Cockade' providing a number of the displays. The press made particular mention of one stand Rotter supplied for the British Iron & Steel Federation, with 'shiny steel surfaces, twisted girders, and perforated metal textures of all kinds'.

Pick also selected one of Gardner's stands for special mention – the Gas Council's '7 Ages of Women' which told the story of the changing use of gas equipment in the home, for which Gardner had Barbara Jones provide a mural. Pick described the whole affair as having the light-hearted touch of a circus or fair.

The 1950 Exhibition catalogue has Charles Truefit as the Daily Mail organizer, with Douglas Dick as that year's architect and Sergei Kadleigh as the consultant architect for the Grand Hall. Over the subsequent years the Grand Hall was to become the main area for designers to unleash their idiosyncratic imaginations. The catalogue described Kadleigh's Grand Hall as 'a masterpiece of silver metallic tracery, unequalled in the past'. *Art & Industry* were equally appreciative calling it 'a lofty citadel of gossamer metalwork and radiant banners'.

Gardner was also involved in dressing the Grand Hall for a number of years. *Display* congratulated him on the 'elegance and economy' of his 1951 offering:

In his bold use of bunting on the grand scale; in the lace-like structure suggestive of the Great Exhibition; in his Victorian colour harmonies; and in the magnificent display effect created by the richly ornate chandeliers [each nearly 30ft. tall]; James Gardner achieves a perfect centennial atmosphere.

Misha Black made a special reference to the Ideal Home Exhibition in his book on exhibitions, albeit with a somewhat caustic comment on the exhibits –

...the solid background of the British furnishing trade being often spiced with the thinly distributed pepper of contemporary design of a very high standard.

And, for the first time in a book on design, we get a number of illustrations of the Ideal Home Exhibition

Various catalogues for the Ideal Home Exhibition, from 1950, 1954 and 1963 (left to right).

of what Black considered 'a very high standard' – two views of Rotter's British Iron & Steel Federation stands for 1948 and 1949; DRU's Gutmann and Frazer stand for 'The Housewife' in 1948; Gardner's British Gas Council stand of 1948; Brian Peake (DRU) for William Perring, the furniture manufacturer; Hugh Casson's design for Sanderson's in 1949; and Kadleigh's remarkable parabola in the Grand Hall for 1950. Other designs illustrated were Christopher Heal's principal feature in the Grand Hall for his furniture firm, and Christopher Ironside and Margaret Casson's jolly stand for Schweppes, with people made out of bottles.

By 1954 Hugh Casson had taken over as consultant for the Grand Hall, working in association with Robin and Christopher Ironside. That year's catalogue again uses violet prose to describe their contribution:

The art of Sir Hugh Casson and his two brilliant associates … has translated the Grand Hall at Olympia into a scene so swiftly imaginative that the mind of every visitor will, surely, be wrenched from a tacit acceptance of the inevitable sameness of life outside and made instantly sensitive to the many new ideas embodied in the thousands of exhibits on every hand.

One can only wonder at the actual effect on the average visitor of Casson's Apollo driving eighteen golden horses fifty feet above the main aisle towards an equally awesome Diana, and its relevance to their terrace dwelling, semi-detached or Metroland bungalow!

In 1993 the Ideal Home Exhibition received, retrospectively, its most important design accolade, when Deborah Ryan mounted a show in its honour at the prestigious Design Museum. It was reported as having more visitors than any show, to that date, at the Museum. But yet again, the focus was on the merchandise that had been exhibited over the years rather than on how they had been exhibited, a missed opportunity for giving due acknowledgement to the many designers, so many unnamed, who had helped make the show such a success for so many years.

PROPAGANDA EXHIBITIONS

A Gallant Enterprise in Adverse Circumstances
(of the Ministry of Information wartime exhibitions)

Although an embryonic Ministry of Information existed towards the end of WWI, government departments were largely responsible for their own 'propaganda' until the beginning of WWII. As early as 1935 planning had started in order to establish a central department in face of the increasingly active Nazi propaganda machine. The Ministry of Information (MoI) came into being the day after war was declared – 4th September 1939; but in spite of the lead time, the birth has generally been assessed as something of a shambles. Duff Cooper was one who described it as such:

...the 'monster' came into existence the day after the outbreak of war and 999 officials sprang to their office chairs ... ex-ambassadors, retired Indian civil servants, briefless barristers – no species of clever amateur was unrepresented.

Within the first year or so there were four different Ministers responsible for MoI, and four different Director Generals operating it; things did not settle down until Churchill found someone he could work with – Brendon Bracken – who began to shape the Ministry and give it some sort of policy and stability. For a very brief period – August to December – Frank Pick, late of London Transport, was administratively in charge. Pick wrote of his appointment:

...it was an unlooked for affair and one that nobody would seek for themselves ... I went in under compulsion.

He went on to account for his short reign, 'My fault was that I acted too slowly and considerately, and this they took for weakness.'

Nevertheless Pick, with his considerable experience of publicity, managed to mount, on the

Previous page and above: Photographs from the Ministry of Information's 'Poison Gas' exhibition. Right: Entrance to the 'Back at Work' exhibition.

suggestion of Christian Barman, an exhibition of photographs on 'Why we are at War'. And it was Pick, supported by Kenneth Clark, who got Milner Gray installed as Head of the Ministry of Information's Exhibition Branch, first to be housed at Senate House, and later, in 1942, to move to Russell Square. Milner Gray was already an established exhibition designer having worked on advertising exhibitions, the MARS Group exhibition, and sections of the British Pavilion at the New York World Fair, amongst other events; and for coordinating designers at the Ministry, he had already had the experience of founding one of the first design groups in the country, initially named Bassett-Gray, and then the Industrial Design Unit (IDU).

At first the Ministry's Exhibition Division consisted solely of Gray and was scathingly referred to as the 'one-man' division. He was faced with the problem of recruiting suitable staff, when being an artist was not a reserved occupation. Additionally there were no college courses on exhibition design to draw from, so he was obliged to fall back on gathering together a mixed group of architects and commercial artists in the hopes that they would gel.

Some of Gray's motley band had work in IDU, as Norbert Dutton (who had been a co-founder), and Kenneth Bayes, an architect who, in the Division came to specialize in temporary structures. Others he drew from a variety of sources, as Peter Ray, who, pre-war, had worked on *Shelf Appeal* and came into the Division to specialize in display typography; Beverley Pick, who had been a window display man, carried this specialism into the Division; and Gordon Cullen, who had been an architectural writer and illustrator, and came to be the Division's expert on display statistics and symbols. Dorothy Goslett, was not only a rare woman to have significance in the Ministry's wartime exhibition work as an administrator, but was later to administrate the Design Research Unit (with Gray and Misha Black at the helm after WWII), and to write the first book on the subject of design administration.

Gray was particularly keen to bring in his IDU colleague, Misha Black, who was actually ineligible to become a civil servant being still a Russian national. Eventually Gray got round this by offering Black a weekly contract as 'consultant architect on the arrangement and lay-out of exhibitions, with special regard to his knowledge of propaganda requirements'. Similarly F.H.K. Henrion, who was not naturalized until 1946, was used as a consultant, becoming particularly involved with work on behalf of the Ministry of Agriculture.

When Gray took on the role of Principal Design Advisor to the Division, a year or so after Clifford Bloxham had taken over as its administrative Head, there was to be a dramatic expansion as Bloxham was something of an empire builder. By 1942, there were over sixty people in the Division, and, for really big projects, many freelance designers were called upon as well, as Jan Lewitt and George Him, Bruce Angrave and Pearl Falconer. Additionally there were a string of copywriters and journalists involved, as George Orwell who worked on several of the Division's exhibitions, as 'Free Europe's Forces', and Robert Sinclair (feature editor of *The Star*) who worked on 'Poison Gas'. The advertising for the Division's exhibitions was mainly handled by an outside agency – Dorland Advertising.

In London, the Ministry's exhibitions were largely mounted in Charing Cross Underground Station. It was there it had its first exhibition – 'London Pride', to be followed by most of the others throughout the war. There were also facilities to show in the foyer of

Left: Photograph from the 'Back at Work' exhibition, showing a disabled worker's capacity to contribute to the war effort.

A general view of the 'Count Your Coupons' exhibition held at Charing Cross Underground Station, 1943.

Dignitaries inspect a map at the 'French Resistance' exhibition organised by the Ministry of Information.

Senate House itself, and occasionally it was used for this purpose. When there was a particular relevance other sites might be employed as with the 1942 'Utility Furniture' exhibition at the Building Centre. Other London venues used were Dorland Hall, the Guildhall, and several shops, as the former Rootes car showroom in Piccadilly, and for no easily explained reason, the premises of James Brook & Sons Ltd in Bethnal Green Road. Possibly some relevance could be argued when the Regents Park Zoo was used for 'Off the Ration', which was not only about growing your own food but keeping <u>animals</u> for food – with live pigs, rabbits and hens, looked after by live land girls, themselves being something of an attraction.

Perhaps the most poignant venue was that of the bombed site of the John Lewis store in Oxford Street. It was as if the Ministry was declaring that however bad the bombing, the Brits would show their grit and determination to win. One of the best-remembered exhibitions on the site was the Army Exhibition of 1944, which was later to tour the country. For this the Royal Engineers constructed underground trenches and an overhead bridge to enable the public, who flocked in, to gain as realistic experience as possible of the army's contribution and the conditions it had to work in.

The Ministry of Information's display scheme for shops was something apart. This was a scheme to

ARMY exhibition

New Street, Birmingham

APRIL 1st to 30th, 1944
DAILY, 10 a.m. to 8 p.m.

Admission free

The exhibition has been produced for the War Office by the Ministry of Information.

Left: Leaflet for the Birmingham installment of the Army Exhibition, 1944. **Right:** The large-scale Army Exhibition held on the bombed site of the John Lewis department store on London's Oxford Street, 1943.

which stores throughout the country could subscribe, whereby the Ministry provided a whole window display provided the shop or store made no use of it for selling its merchandise. The first of these displays was sent out in July 1940, to some three hundred stores, the montage supplied by McKnight Kauffer, with a large photo of the Prime Minister and the slogan 'Hold fast and we win'. Many others followed, publicising the work of the various forces as well as the Home Front, from which came such slogans as 'Up Housewives and at 'Em'.

The earliest Ministry of Information exhibitions were largely concerned with keeping up morale, and instructing people as to how to behave in air raids when they did occur. 'London Pride' had shown how people were learning to cope in London, trying to carry on as near normally as they could; but there were also exhibitions on ways of coping with possible effects of bombing as 'How to fight the Fire Bomb', and the dramatic 'Poison Gas' with its iconic poster by F.H.K. Henrion and such displays of 'how to apply anti-gas cream' and 'how to wash, if splashed with blister gas'. Although 'Poison Gas' had alarming elements to it, it also had more reassuring ones, as how a gas mask actually works

Left: Banner at the Army Exhibition, Oxford Street, London, 1943. **Opposite left:** MoI exhibition, 'Victory Over Japan' (designer, Beverley Pick). **Opposite right:** Installation at the MoI's 'Dig for Victory' exhibition (designers, Milner Gray, Misha Black and Peter Ray).

others encouraged self-sufficiency as 'Dig for Victory' (designed by Gray, Misha Black and Peter Ray) – a title that was to become part of common parlance and which ensured that every available scrap of land was to be given over to growing food; the 'Domestic Front' with instructional exhibits as to how to maintain a sound diet accompanied by cookery demonstrations on how to make the most of dried eggs, and similar topics. Being economic, as with clothes and furnishings, was met with exhibitions with titles such as 'Make and Mend' and 'Count your Coupons', covering such concerns as how to conserve one's wardrobe, how to combat moths, how to recycle old clothes, and how to make the most of that 'little black dress'. The housewife was given a key role as fighter on the Home Front – not only planting and sewing, but salvaging, and a number of exhibitions were devoted to linking savings on the Home Front directly to munitions, as 'Private Scrap Builds a Bomber' and 'Private Scrap goes to the Front'.

And along with the housewife battling in the home and garden, there were exhibitions showing the contribution being made by other sections of the community, demonstrating how everybody was 'pulling together'. Examples are 'Life-Line' which covered

and there were facilities for having one's own mask checked.

By 1942 the Exhibition Division was in full swing and more than a dozen exhibitions were mounted that year. In addition to a focus on how the public could help themselves there was, by now, the additional concern as to how they could either directly, or indirectly, help the troops. Along with 'Off the Ration', which was designed by Milner Gray, Bronek Katz and F.H.K. Henrion, a number of the role of the Merchant Navy, demonstrating their particular courage in dealing with mines and torpedoes in order to bring in necessary supplies; the 'London Fire Brigade and Auxiliary Fire Service' and the 'Firewatcher'; and the contribution disabled people were making, people who had been considered of little use to the economy but now shown to have relevant skills. 'Back to Work' had people, handicapped in various ways, demonstrating their actual capabilities. And an even larger group – women – considered 'too fragile' for so many jobs in peacetime – had their strengths demonstrated, particularly in relation to munitions work, by such exhibitions as 'Women's War Work'.

It was considered increasingly important also to get the public to appreciate the contribution of allied forces. It might seem incredulous to that younger generation who were to live through the Cold War, or the current youth, faced with varied international prejudices and suspicions, to learn that the British Government, in its time, put on such exhibitions as '25 Years of the USSR and the Red Army' and 'Comrades in Arms' – showing the lives of Russian civilians and troops; and 'The Story of Lin; a picture of China at War' – mounted with the aid of the Chinese equivalent of the Ministry of Information. Of course Britain's more 'natural' allies were feted as well, with 'Meet Canada', 'John Olsson – the story of

an average American', 'America Marches' and 'Free Europe's Forces', and the like, the last celebrating refugees from occupied countries who were contributing contingents fighting alongside the British Forces, as the Poles and the French. By 1943 exhibitions were increasingly focused on what was happening beyond Europe – 'Jungle Front', 'Our Eastern Job' and 'Ocean Front' all covered the war in the Pacific.

The general tone of all the Division's exhibitions was morale boosting – how great we were, how important our values are, and if we all push together we will win through. Only the odd exhibition indulged in negative propaganda – playing on how weak and despicable was our enemy, as 'How Italy lost her Empire' and 'The Nazi Way of Life'.

Generally the press were positive about the Ministry's wartime exhibitions. A typical example was the *Architectural Review* which gave 'top marks for a government department'. Avril Black in her book on Milner Gray was to be particularly

extravagant in her praise of the wartime Ministry of Information exhibitions:

...so successful that they set the pace for all major exhibition designs in the western world after the war, notably the Festival of Britain.

Certainly they were a success if the criterion of number of visitors they attracted is used. A counting device, installed at Charing Cross, marked up 66,252 visitors to 'America Marches' in the 25 days of its run; 'Off the Ration', running for some 61 days, attracted about half a million people; and for a provincial showing in Doncaster of 'The Nazi Way of Life' as many as 54,000 attended in 8 days. But the winner, by far, not only because of the extent of its touring outside London, but because of the reality of its displays, was 'The Army' which, in all, attracted some three and a half million visitors.

One aspect of having a limited number of objects to exhibit was the increased use of photography, particularly experimentation with photomontage, that was to become a main communication medium in post-war exhibitions; another was the development of the exhibition narrative, of using a story line to explain quite complex situations simply, which was possibly what Blake was considering when linking

wartime exhibition developments to what was to be involved in the design of the Festival of Britain. Milner Gray, himself, was to recall 'The sparse-narrative discipline of those days', which he felt had been seen at its best in 'America Marches', and which was, shortly after the war finished, to be used in various of the Council of Industrial Design exhibitions, most prominently in 'Britain Can Make It'.

These wartime exhibitions, by their sheer number, and by the conditions under which they were produced, gave the designers involved, some relatively inexperienced in exhibition work, the groundwork for their post-war exhibition commissions i.e. the ability and flexibility to produce creative solutions under time pressure within tight budgets.

DESIGN
EXHIBITIONS

Designers, as a combined force, seem to have generally lacked the confidence and the clout to mount exhibitions themselves, to any great extent. When they did manage to form any sort of 'union', as with the founding of the Society of Industrial Artists in 1930, they were largely preoccupied with matters of status, training, salaries and conditions of work, rather than spreading concepts of 'good design' through public exhibitions. The very fact that SIA's founding members were skewed towards 'fine' art, and even the early minority of 'design' members tended towards 'graphics' rather than 'industry', also seems to have set the tone of the Society. Generally if SIA chose to spread the gospel it would be through conferences, lectures and publications rather than exhibitions; and when it occasionally did dip its toe into such shows the contribution seems to have been a rather modest one. Exhibitions, encouraging better designed products and improved consumer taste,

seem to have come about when industrialists put their weight behind the idea.

Royal Society of Arts Exhibitions

Design-orientated exhibitions, aiming at increasing the appreciation of good design, both in manufacturers and in the buying public, started as early as the 18th century when the Royal Society of Arts, Manufacture and Commerce (now RSA) was founded. The RSA claims to have mounted the first ever public exhibition in this country, in 1760; and, in the following year, the first industrial exhibition of agricultural machinery. However, it was not until the mid-19th century it linked art with industry in a series of small exhibitions encouraged by Prince Albert; and these in turn were to trigger the Great Exhibition of 1851. RSA's 'Select Specimens of British Manufacturers and Decorative Art' (1847) attracted

more than 20,000 visitors, albeit it is said that manufacturers had to be bullied to produce sufficient
exhibits. There then seems to have been a gap of
some eighty years, during which RSA's proselytizing
took the form of competitions, awards, lectures and
publications, before it again mounted an exhibition
specifically encouraging good design, when, in 1935,
it joined forces with the Royal Academy with what
Art & Industry described as 'an air of vague benevo-
lence' for 'British Art & Industry', held at Burlington
House. Royalty again was involved with the then

Prince of Wales, Vice-Patron of the RSA, agreeing
to become President of the Committee for the
Exhibition. What was termed the Exhibition General
Committee was overloaded with Lords and Ladies,
and the odd Marquis. Its Executive Committee

had six RA representatives, including Lutyens and Gilbert Scott, and six RSA representatives, including Tom Purvis.

In his foreword to 'The Story of the Royal Society of Arts', published in 1935, J.A. Milne optimistically described this cooperative effort:

The two great Institutions representing fine and industrial art respectively, being entirely independent and free from anything in the way of 'vested interests', are in a position to hold an Exhibition such as this from an entirely altruistic standpoint and with one view only; namely to stimulate artists, manufacturers and the public generally to appreciate a beautiful thing, even if the machine enters mainly into its composition ... The Exhibition, taking place in the galleries of the Royal Academy, transforms them into a wonderful display of objects and materials excellent in design and contemporary in execution and is expected to create world-wide interest ... it may lay the foundation for the future, the results of which may be far-reaching.

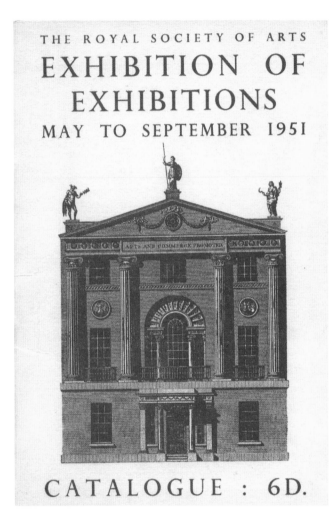

THE ROYAL SOCIETY OF ARTS

EXHIBITION OF EXHIBITIONS

MAY TO SEPTEMBER 1951

CATALOGUE : 6D.

Catalogue from the RSA's contribution to the Festival of Britain: 'Exhibition of Exhibitions', 1951.

As was inevitable, when exhibition exhibits were chosen by an elite committee, paranoia set in. A letter to the organizing secretary was typical:

I have met craftsmen who are frightened by the list of gentlemen who form the executive committee to whom the final selection is reserved. Distinguished gentlemen but not specially qualified to deal with matters of this sort … their names do not inspire confidence in the minds of those who have for many years now laboured for an improvement in design in industry.

The Exhibition was something of a gamble for both organisations, not only because the Royal Academy was unused to mounting such a display, but because it was a financial risk, as exhibitors were not charged and there was no government subsidy. The Exhibition was divided into eleven product sections – ceramics, glassware, silver and clocks etc. – and in addition there were shop windows – display windows, with changing occupants, over the period of the Exhibition.

Display was generally positive in its reporting, perhaps because the 'show windows' provided a rare prestige moment for displaymen to show off. It found the ceramics section to have 'a tone of quietness and simplicity' with plain moldings for the frames and pillars showing off the exhibits. Although it thought that things were a little overcrowded, generally it considered that the Exhibition provided a valuable object lesson in how to use different size and shape of settings to show off goods to the best effect. Of the 'shop windows' it specifically named

The SIA's exhibition for the Cotton Board, 'Colour, Design & Style Centre', 1951.

as oustanding Selfridge's winter sports display, and Martha Harris's display of Tootal handkerchiefs. Its major criticism was about colour, or lack of it, and how lighting failed to bring out what colour there was – the 'plastics' being too dull, and the furnishing fabrics not lit to effect. Colour was, again, a matter for complaint, in *Commercial Art*, which curiously

sent Wyndham Lewis along to record his reactions. He did not hold back:

There are no colours properly speaking, but only biscuit, buff, gull's-egg grey, light fawn, faded horizon blue...

But Lewis's main complaint was about the 'slickness' of it all; in this he was perhaps commenting rather about the exhibits themselves, than how they had been displayed. He searched in vain 'for an uncompromising corner or a good stiff right-angle' – everything was too curved for him. *Commercial Art*, perhaps in an attempt to balance Lewis's forthrightness, also provided comments from those actually involved in the Exhibition – manufacturers and designers, but, again, these were rather more on the exhibits. *The Journal* provides a rare account of an exhibition designer going about her job – one Mrs. Darcy Braddell designing a show kitchen:

I certainly kept the aesthetic aspect of the room very much in mind, as otherwise the objects themselves are unlikely to attract sufficient interest from an ordinary 'exhibition' public, unless they are demonstrated or have written descriptions [which I knew was not the case] ... [of manufacturers] In some cases it was only necessary for me to give ideas and conditions, and they then showed much enterprise and ability in meeting the situation. In other cases they needed considerably more from me than mere suggestions.

One first, for the Exhibition, was the affixing of the designer's name to his or her object, which was considered an important breakthrough by the design profession. But this did not seem to apply to the display designers, themselves, who were rarely mentioned by name, even in the design press. Whether Milne's prediction that the Exhibition would 'lay a foundation for the future' is questionable, albeit some commentators have suggested that it stirred the government to set up the Council for Art and Industry, that was, in concept, to eventually morph into the Council of Industrial Design.

Design & Industries Association Exhibitions

The Design & Industries Association was founded in 1915, triggered by concern for the likely effect of the war on trade and the fact that German manufacturing and industrial design was far ahead of our own:

What is needed at the present time is the gathering together of all the several interests concerned with industrial production into a closer association; an association of manufacturers, designers, distributors, economists, and critics ... a closer contact between branches of production and distribution ... and a need to explain its aim and ideals to the public.

DIA's early members included the printers, Harold Curwen and Fred Phillips, the designer Gregory Brown, the textile manufacturer, James Morton and the educationalist Fred Burridge, who had succeeded Lethaby at the Central School of Arts & Crafts. With an eagerness to proselytize, which

Fiona McCarthy has termed 'high-mindedness', DIA mounted several exhibitions, as one in conjunction with the Board of Trade held at the Goldsmith's Hall during WWI, with the declared aim:

...to encourage a more intelligent demand amongst the public for what is best and soundest in design.

For this, DIA members were said to have combed shops, and even their own homes, for well-designed German and Austrian goods, presumably to show up the shoddiness of British goods in comparison.

DIA's 'Design and Workmanship in Print' was also put on in 1915, at the Whitechapel Art Gallery, attracting some 30,000 visitors and, later, travelling to provincial art galleries. With a couple of small further exhibitions under its belt – a 1916 one held at the Royal Academy (where commercially manufactured goods were on show for the first time) and 'Homes for Heroes', put on in 1919 – DIA held a rather more ambitious show, again at the Whitechapel Art Gallery – 'Household Things', consisting of a series of rooms, and some special sections on cooking and heating, many of the exhibits again lent by DIA members.

After this heady start DIA calmed its early enthusiasm for exhibitions, particularly in the face of slump and unemployment, and retreated, as it were, to its offices in Queen's Square, where it, nevertheless, kept a large room available for exhibitions, including two on textiles and on printing. The 1930s brought fewer exhibitions and a greater focus on conferences, developing regional networks,

DESIGN IN BRITISH GOODS

DIA 'Design in British Goods', Charing Cross
Underground Station, London, 1932.

and publications such as the *DIA Yearbook*, begun
in 1922, its 'Quarterly Journal' edited by Noel
Carrington, to be followed by *Design in Industry*.

The DIA did, indirectly, contribute to other small
exhibitions, in that some of its members contributed
to a 'British Industrial Art in Relation to the Home'
exhibition, held at the Dorland Hall; and also some
small exhibitions, held in some of the department
stores, had DIA members select the exhibits. And
it rather pompously responded, when invited to
mount a DIA section in 1938, for a 'Women's Fair &
Exhibition' at Olympia, perhaps to cover the fact that
they had not previously been particularly active in
using exhibitions to get their message across:

*For the first time ... a group of Associations con-
cerned with Art, Science, Education and Industry,
has been invited to participate in a great National
Exhibition with the object of investing it with a
SOCIAL PURPOSE.*

Curiously it was the onset of war, when manufacturing had other concerns and exhibits were likely to
be scarce, that DIA was stirred to mount exhibitions
again – Noel Carrington and Elizabeth Denby putting
on 'Homes to Live In' and John Grey and Marjorie
Morrison one entitled 'Design Round the Clock'.

After the war, in the 1950s DIA had two exhibitions, both held at Charing Cross Underground
Station, where they tried to involve the public
actively – 'Register Your Choice' in 1953 in which
visitors were presented with two rooms, (one
furnished to DIA taste and the other to the taste
of the National Association of Retail Furnishers),
and asked to vote for that which they preferred; and
in 1957 DIA put on a similar exhibition – 'Make or
Mar'. But by the 1950s the government had become
altogether more active for the cause of 'design in
industry', and non-governmental bodies largely took
a back seat when it came to exhibitions.

Government Sponsored Design Exhibitions

It took the British government some time to fully appreciate that 'good design meant good business', and
when they did, their concern was consequently made
the responsibility of the Board of Trade. As early as

1908, the Board of Trade had set up an Exhibition Branch, largely concerning itself with increasing exports, and, therefore, exhibitions abroad. By the start of WWI, a more full-blooded stance was adopted to educate all concerned with the manufacture, distribution and purchase of goods as to the importance of improving design, but converting plans to action had to be delayed during the war, and it was not until 1920 that the government was able to launch its British Institute of Industrial Art (BIIA). The cynical lampooned it as being 'a Purgatory, for the crystallising of taste'.

The government had part funded some of the DIA's small proganada exhibitions of German manufactured goods, but now, through BIIA, mounted several exhibitions, mainly at the Victoria & Albert Museum, with such titles as 'Modern Crafts and Manufacturers' (1920), 'Present Day Industrial Art' (1922). 'Industrial Art Today' (1923) and 'Industrial Art for the Slender Purse' (1929). But this early flush of enthusiasm was reined in with the economic downturn of the late '20s, and, with the government gradually cutting back funding; BIIA was eventually dissolved in 1934.

But the government hadn't entirely lost interest in the cause of furthering good design, and the Board of Trade set up a Committee, under the chairmanship of Lord Gorrell, to report on 'the production and exhibition of articles of good design and everyday use'. The Gorrell Report was published in 1932. Although it argued, that, in the long-run, a prestige

Left: 'Design Fair' leaflet for a travelling CoID exhibition, 1948, (designer, James Gardner). **Right:** Part of a detailed plan for a travelling display for the CoID (designer, Donald Bell-Scott).

building in the centre of London would be desirable for exhibiting good design, it realized that this would not immediately be practical, and so focused its main recommendations on having a coordinated policy for major exhibitions of industrial art in the hands of 'a central controlling body' that could handle the mounting of exhibitions 'with tact and discretion and with the definite object of improving manufactured goods'. Although the Committee gave a nod to out-of-London, and to travelling exhibitions, there was a clear metropolitan bias to its recommendations, and a similar elitism was shown in its recommendations as to membership of this controlling body:

Although we recommend the inclusion on the central body of a few members with experience of manufacture, wholesale trade and retail trade, members should be primarily chosen not as representing particular sections of the community, but as persons of taste and cultural standards, with an up-to-date, and as far as possible, an international outlook on Art.

This potential 'cosiness' and 'cronyism' of the proposed body's membership was somewhat tempered by some slightly more egalitarian recommendations – that every article exhibited should bear the name of the designer as well as that of the manufacturer;

that every effort should be made to break down the barrier between 'fine' and 'industrial' art; and that exhibitions mounted by the central body should show 'really beautiful (though cheap) goods of modern design'. When one considers that the Committee included Roger Fry (with his 'exquisite' experiments

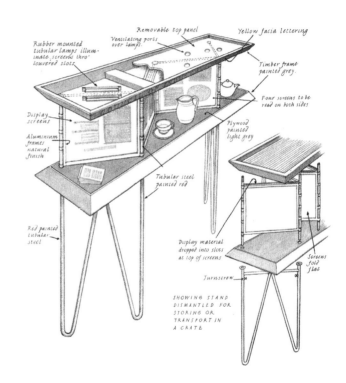

DESIGNER'S DRAWING
Designed by DONALD BELL-SCOTT—part of detailed drawing of a
travelling display for the Council of Industrial Design
Dimensions: 6 ft. 2 in. × 1 ft. 6 in. × 5 ft. 6 in. high

'War to Peace' section, BCMI exhibition, 1946 (designer, Beverley Pick).

at the Omega Workshop), Clough Williams-Ellis (with his bizarre ideas on architecture) and Professor E.W. Tristram, a mediaevalist who 'did not find it possible to attend any of the Committee's meetings', Gorrell, perhaps, is to be congratulated at having come out with a workable scheme as a result of which the Council for Art and Industry (CoAI) came into being, with Frank Pick, only recently taking up the appointment of Vice-Chairman and Chief Executive of LPTB, as Chair. And, indeed, the CoAI came to be known as 'Pick's Committee'.

In fact Pick's Committee was only able to put on a few exhibitions before the onset of WWII, some small exhibitions at the V&A between 1934 and 1936, and an exhibition of low-cost rooms, held at the Building Centre in 1937, and, of notoriety, a not very impressive contribution to the Paris Exhibition of the same year. Nevertheless its heart was in the right place for an unpublished Council report recommended:

...the time has come to institute an active exhibition policy in this country, in the hope that if regular

and comprehensive arrangements were made to show the public (including manufacturers and distributors) the best specimens of industrial production, a healthy stimulus would be given to industry, as well as to art and technical schools, and sound standards of design would gradually be established.

Pick's Committee had to suspend its work with the onset of WWII, and a voluntary body came into being – the Council of Industrial Art & Design – to protect the interests of the various organisations concerned with design during the war. But by 1943, the government was beginning to consider the possible post-war economy and the role of design, and this resulted in the Post-War Export Trade Committee on Industrial Design and Art in Industry (the Weir Committee) and the Meynell-Haskin Report. As a result, the Council of Industrial Design (CoID) was established – 'to promote by all practical means the improvement of design in the products of British Industry' – by exhibitions, product endorsement and an advisory service. Although it was not to open Gorrell's 'permanent building' until 1956 – the Design Centre – the CoID lost no time in mounting one of the most significant industrial design orientated exhibitions – 'Britain Can Make It' (BCMI).

'Britain Can Make It'

...a vision, a succession of scenes each one obviously created by an artist, and all coordinated and controlled within a simple conception. There were no advertising names, no sales talk in panels; design was paramount.
John Nicholson, *Rumble*, Crowther & Nicholas

'Britain Can Make It', held at the V&A in 1946, can probably be rated a key exhibition when it comes to prosyletising design, albeit not an entirely successful one. Of course, different interested parties had varying motives for putting on such a show, with such a short lead time and such limited resources. The government, represented by Sir Stafford Cripps, was largely concerned with the revival of the British economy, particularly its export trade. Cripps, being as James Gardner described him, 'an intellectual and a visionary', had the optimism to hope that such an exhibition would raise the standard of design in British manufacturing; the CoID, the new broom, was eager to prove itself, to show its energy and imagination in this its first major show; and then there was also an element of cheering up the war exhausted population, the need to build a spirit of optimism as to the 'brave new world', a need that was to be more effectively met by the Festival of Britain. And, as with the Festival, there were the designers, many of them young and testing their talents, others, who had been involved in war work, now wanting to re-establish themselves. It was to be the first exhibition commissioned for the recently established Design Research Unit, to make or break the new enterprise, luckily the former. And indeed, it was the first major exhibition for James

Gardner, who, for some reason was appointed the Exhibitions Chief Display Designer, possibly because of his maverick high jinx in Camouflage during the war, as he had had little more experience of exhibitions, other than some small projects for Jack Beddington at Shell. Gardner's facetious record of his work for the Exhibition, which he called 'all Barnum and Bailey', belied his quiet, meticulous contribution.

With rationing of materials, and the resultant scarcity of things to exhibit, it is praiseworthy that the exhibition was mounted at all. Although Cripp's instructions were 'to design a show that would look complete in every detail even if we didn't get exhibits', there were reports of manufacturers grumbling about the 'central in-group' who controlled the selection of exhibits, with its 'metropolitan bias'; nevertheless Dudley Ryder, Chief Exhibitions Officer of the CoID, felt able to write that 'the support received by the Council from manufacturers was remarkable considering the difficulties'.

The exhibition was in sections, each with its own appointed designer or group of designers and each focusing on a specific group of products, along with more educational sections, as the entrance 'War to Peace', showing how technical developments in wartime were now being applied to consumer products, and 'What the Goods are Made of', to the most publicized section on the design process itself, Misha Black's and DRU's 'What Industrial Design Means' – where an egg cup was used as an example!

Above: Misha Black's 'egg cup' from the design process section of the BCMI exhibition, 1946.
Right: Lewitt-Him's (Jan Lewitt and George Him) stand for Travel Goods, BCMI, 1946.

Generally, those involved in mounting the Exhibition appear to have been pleased with their efforts. Cripps was particularly effusive:

The Council of Industrial Design has done a good job for British Industry, and so have all those manufacturers and workers who have co-operated with them in this Exhibition. This is not the end, but rather the beginning, I hope, of an ever improving standard of design in all the goods we make and sell.

Ryder seems to have been equally pleased:

During the war we were starved of colour and decoration, and in this Exhibition light and colour were used to a large extent and mural artists engaged when decoration was required, instead of covering the wall surfaces with large black and white photographs.

Gardner, when asked for his opinion, in retrospect, merely replied that things would have been worse without BCMI, but that it didn't have the impact it should have had. The press gave it a more mixed reception. *Art & Industry* called it 'a triumph of showmanship' and declared that 'this Exhibition demonstrated not only that "Britain Can Make It" but that "Britain Can Design It".' Henry Trethowan, of Heal's, similarly referred to it as 'a Triumph in Presentation'; and John Gloag, the design commentator, expressed his glee that 'we finally got over the Victorian hangover in design'.

However, there was a certain amount of displeasure shown by some designers, not only about the difficulty of getting sufficient exhibits, but that so many were not available to the home market. Milner

Gray wrote somewhat cynically that it was:

...a large shop where you had to pay for the privilege of going in, knowing in advance that you wouldn't be allowed to buy the goods when you got in there ... [yet they stood] hour after hour on the Kensington pavement.

Nearly one and a half million people visited the show. DRU attempted to gauge visitors' opinions with 'Quiz Banks' and 'Quiz Books'. Mass Observation, approaching the whole question of validity rather more professionally, reported that 80% really enjoyed the exhibition (only 2% rating it bad), but that most did not feel their tastes had been

changed by what they had seen. Very few even made mention of the section 'What Industrial Design Means', possibly wincing at what the Blakes termed 'coating educational pills with whimsy'.

Although BCMI has been fairly extensively researched, written about, and archived (at the University of Brighton Design Archives), from the viewpoint of an exhibition design historian there are still a number of fuzzy areas – what, if any, was Ryder's contribution; why was Gardner chosen when Spence, seeming to have a lesser role, yet to be clearly spelt out, had the greater experience; why

has so little space been given to the various section designers, apart from Black's, when some of the other sectional displays merit more than a mention, as Beverley Pick's 'War into Peace', Robert Goodden's sports section, and Lewitt-Him's whimsical section displaying luggage; and why has so little been made of the murals and paintings, including those by Hans Feibusch, Laurence Scarfe, Barbara Jones, Vanessa Bell, Duncan Grant and Victor Pasmore, and to what extent they enhanced the exhibits.

Jonathan Woodham, in his book on BCMI concluded that as a result of the exhibition:

...although a number of lessons have been learned through bitter experience, it was clear that the evangelical message of Good Design was easier to preach than to radically influence either industrial or social attitudes.

Although CoID, through its Scottish Committee mounted 'Enterprise Scotland' in the following year, this seems to have been rather more of a celebratory exhibition aimed at export and the tourist trade, than one focusing on 'design'. Gardner and Spence were the main designers, Spence for overall layout and Gardner titled as Chief, the displays being provided by Cockade. *Art & Industry* were effusive:

...lavishly using vast quantities of woven material they achieve that exciting atmosphere of an unusually sumptuous 'big top', with all the lights of the fair thrown in, giving a feeling of exhilaration all too lacking in these gloomy days...

Display even more so:

Left: Industrial design model of a caravan, BCMI, 1946 (designer, John Ensor). **Above:** Jacques Groag's furnishing fabric display, BCMI, 1946.

89

The 'Men's Wear' section of the BCMI exhibition, 1946 (designer, Ashley Havinden).

There are abstract shapes, there are unorthodox compositions, there are unusual colours in unexpected places but most of these can truly be described as vehicles for the expression of a story, not as mere decorative whim. Frills and fol de lols introduced for their own sake are not apparent; the complicated curlicue and the deckle-edged dado are left where they belong – at the bottom of the property box!

'Enterprise Scotland', held in the Royal Scottish Museum, Edinburgh, was only one third of the size of BCMI, although it allowed itself to spill out on to Princes Street, with fourteen retailers also involved. Although there were amazing effects as an 18ft figure – Jenny Weave – draped in tartan, a 25ft St. Andrew suspended from the central dome, and 6,000 yards of glass cloth draping the Hall of Pinnacles, that is there were some awe-inspiring designs, there was little directly educational on the design process and the importance of design as there had been in BCMI, albeit Gardner had a display on the exhibition story, showing how the exhibition was organized.

However, in 1948, CoID combined forces with RSA, to again put 'design' first, with the exhibition 'Design at Work', showing off products mainly designed by the RSA's Royal Designers of Industry (RDI), the elite of industrial art, each rated at the top of their respective field. The booklet accompanying the exhibition described its intent:

…the exhibition shows how the designer is the co-ordinating link in a team which includes the manufacturer, management, technician, wholesaler and retailer, and by no means least, the consumer.

The Exhibition was held at Burlington House, *Art & Industry* described it briefly:

The whole anatomy of the subject [industrial design] is skilfully exposed in a series of factual case histories ranging from the design of a jet aircraft to textiles and tea-pots…

The overall design of the Exhibition was very much a DRU affair, with Milner Gray as a chief designer assisted by a number of his DRU associates, many of them RDI, with the general management of the project in the capable hands of Dorothy Goslett. Other names associated with 'Design at Work' are Gordon Russell, who chaired the Exhibition Executive Committee, his brother, R.D Russell, Robert Goodden, and, of course, James Gardner pops up yet again.

The Exhibition was spread over four rooms, largely with mixed exhibits, but with Room 3 displaying posters and Room 4, book design. The RSA had its own space to record the part it had played in the progress of industrial design. The 'case histories', of the design process, were illustrated by models, prototypes, job sheets, blueprints, and other relevant documents. Examples included a Wedgwood teapot by Kenneth Murray, utility furniture by Gordon Russell, a tube station by Charles Holden, Milner Gray's packaging for Ilford, and James Gardner's portrayal of a jet plane – altogether more complex and exciting than an egg-cup!

An example of how the case history method was used was Wells Coate's wireless set – from an introductory panel of the manufacturer's brief (cost, size, materials, the parts involved etc.), and on to the designer's preliminary sketches and the construction of prototypes, with various modifications, and detailing the progression of the design over some two and a half years with records of correspondence, phone calls, consultations, and so on. It was an altogether more 'grown-up', less whimsical affair than BCMI, more a matter of informing reasonably intelligent, interested visitors, than preaching down.

Cynically it is more than probable that the general populous developed an improved interest in design via the Ideal Home Exhibitions rather than by those exhibitions setting out directly to influence taste. Of course, much had been achieved by the wartime Utility Scheme, without any direct intent to improve taste, whereby people were virtually forced to discard the frills and furbelows and adapt to simplicity; and, in the event, it came down to retailers, as Habitat and later IKEA, and for the better heeled, Heals and Dunns, to actually bring about a heightened awareness of well designed and well-constructed consumer goods, and their arrangement in the home.

PARIS
1937

EXHIBITING
OURSELVES ABROAD

England has always held herself aloof from the world's opinions. Her responsibility as a world state, as the European partner of a great Empire, and as a trading community with world-wide interests, alike, demand that she should set herself to throw a true and modern picture of her qualities on the screen of the world's mind.
Stephen Tallents, 1955

...all International Exhibitions which seek official recognition must first submit an application to the controlling body.
Bureau International des Expositions

A three-sided cream box, cluttered up with ninety per-cent rubbish as far as product design, display, typography and 'stand design' are concerned, it looked worse than a third-rate backstreet window. This apparently is all that British Industry and the
Board of Trade together could manage to produce to represent Britain...*
W.M. de Majo at the Chicago Trade Fair, 1959

In the fifty or so years covered by this book there were literally dozens of major international exhibitions mounted across the world, and countless minor and trade orientated ones. From the Paris 'Exposition Internationale des Arts Decoratifs et Industriels Modernes' in 1925 to Expo 70 in Japan, there were countless opportunities for Britain to 'project' itself. So busy did the international calendar become, that, as early as 1912, there was a concerted effort by governments to place some kind of brake on the proliferation of international exhibitions, presumably because of the considerable expense involved. In 1928, the Bureau of International Exhibitions (BIE) was founded to oversee the calendar – the bidding and the selection – and to establish

Previous page: Montage of images from the Paris International Exhibition, 1937 (from the cover of the July issue of *Display*, 1937). **Above:** British Pavilion at the Brussels International Exposition, 1935.

some kind of regulatory framework for cooperation between participants. In spite of this it is recorded that a number of countries broke ranks when they felt a particular need to boost exports and tourism.

The British government seems generally to have been a shade less enthusiastic about international appearances than those of other countries, and were slow to appreciate the political, as well as the commercial, benefits of such shindigs, and, when we did venture overseas, our civil servants tended to keep a stern eye on what was displayed and what was spent. Even as early as the 1925 Paris Exhibition *The Building News* was complaining of how backward the British Pavilion was compared to the 'modernity' of those of other nations. Noel Carrington, in the 1930s, commented on the government's attitudes which could well have contributed to such criticism:

Reluctantly the Treasury agrees to go into these exhibitions, because everyone else is going, but determined to keep its pockets well-buttoned-up.

And both Misha Black and Basil Spence were to complain that, when it was a trade-orientated exhibition, the British Pavilion tended to be an 'uncoordinated mass of individual exhibits'; and about shows for what Tallents would term the 'projection of England', that design by government committee would tend to produce 'bland generalisations'.

The Department of Overseas Trade, under the joint control of the Foreign Office and the Board of Trade tended to be the responsible body for overseeing British contributions to major international exhibitions. By the late 1930s it chose to be advised on design aspects by the Central Council for Art & Industry, and, in the post-war years by the Council of Industrial Design (to become the Design Council).

Exhibiting ourselves overseas could take a number of forms, as when we took part in exhibitions or fairs mounted by other governments, as with the New York Fair of 1939, or when we, ourselves, took what tended to be small, largely trade, but sometimes design-orientated exhibitions abroad, as with the British Trade Fair in Stockholm, 1962, and the Festival of British Design in Zurich, 1953, or when Willy de Majo instigated a touring exhibition of eight leading British designers around the United States.

Quite apart from the financial issues of whether the investment was worth the pay-off, and the political considerations of how we should present ourselves to different cultures, there were actual practical considerations of construction and transportation – whether to have most of the display constructed in this country with, what Beverley Pick referred to as 'brazing all the hazards of long distance transportation' (as when it was decided to design and construct in London an Atomic Power Exhibition to be mounted in Geneva), or to rely on contractors in the country where the exhibition was to take place, which Pick described as 'putting ourselves at the mercy of local labour and their often doubtful proficiency', quite apart from our general reluctance, as a nation, to become fluent in the language of another.

Three examples will perhaps sufficiently illustrate the challenges of taking part in international exhibitions, with both failures and triumphs resulting. Our contribution to the Exposition Internationale des Arts et Techniques dans La Vie Moderne, held in Paris in 1937, falls largely into the former category. The French were 'modernists', and much of the Trocadero site today contains remains of the 1937 Exhibition. Much has been made of the fact that the German and Russian Pavilions confronted each other across the site, and of the Spanish Pavilion containing Picasso's 'Guernica', but what of the British?

La Pavilion du Royaume Uni was publicized in a catalogue designed by Ravilious. The building itself

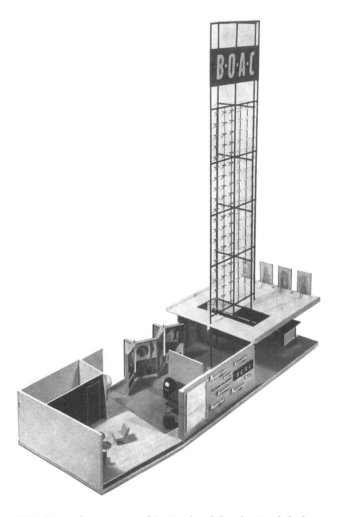

BOAC stand constructed in England for the Baghdad Trade Fair (designer, Beverley Pick).

95

was designed by Oliver Hill, already an established modernist architect (designer of Morecombe's Midland Hotel in 1932), and who had already worked on several exhibitions, including two held at the Dorland Hall in 1933 and '34, on modernism in the home. For Paris he not only designed the British Pavilion, under the watchful eye of Frank Pick, but was also involved in designing displays and selecting the exhibits. A Design & Industries Association Newsletter in 1938, recounted, somewhat facetiously, their relationship:

No sooner appointed First Chairman of the Board of Trade's new Art and Industry Council then he [Pick] summoned Hill to be his right-hand Man of Action. Hence Pick and Hill worked hand-in-glove over the British Pavilion for the Paris International Exhibition of 1937.

Pick wrote of their intent:

Our object throughout has been to stage in the somewhat limited space available, an exhibit of outstanding merit which, with ... scenes typical of various phases of life in the British Isles [will represent] a true conspectus of British Life and civilization.

'British Life' seems to have been skewed towards middle class leisure activities including yachting, flying, caravanning – and weekend houses. Misha Black seemed to start off praising the result as 'an intelligent coherent picture of the British way of life', but followed this with 'albeit the way of life that only 5% of the population can afford'. Carrington, likewise, wrote that although the 'foreigner would be agreeably surprised at the extent and quality of our achievement' BUT that it was by no means a complete picture – 'no business was represented, nor the working class flat, to take two extremes'.

The Press was not so charitable calling it 'a ramshackle affair', with the etched Britannia at the entrance 'from further away looking like Mahatma Ghandi'. *Display* was particularly critical:

To our disgust and shame this is undoubtedly the worst individual effort ... the exterior presenting a ludicrous contrast to the generally excellent buildings presented by other countries ... No British subject with any appreciation of design can fail to experience a sense of shame when he sees this ill-conceived structure...

Book Exhibit in the British Pavilion at the Paris International Exhibition, 1937.

Reception centre seen from the top of the Atomium, Brussels World's Fair, 1958 (Expo 58).

Even Carrington questioned Hill siting the Pavilion entrance away from the Seine – 'Our Pavilion should have opened up with terraces and restaurants to the river front'. Eventually such grumbling led to questions being asked in the House as to the way government money had been so poorly expended (albeit the Treasury had only allowed £35,000 for the Pavilion and its displays). Towards the end of the war, the government, possibly still smarting about the Paris criticism, but certainly concerned about the depleted export trade, in 1945 appointed Lord Ransden to chair a committee:

...to consider the part which exhibitions and fairs should play in the promotion of the export trade in the post-war era, and to advise on the policy and plans to be adopted to derive the maximum advantage from such displays.

This committee was not specifically concerned with international exhibiting but nevertheless, along with its recommendation that the government should continue to support the annual British Industries Fair, it recommended that an International Exhibition should be held in London at the earliest possible date; a recommendation not followed up.

A second example of our exhibiting ourselves overseas was when James Gardner was given free rein for the Brussels Universal and International Exhibition, known as Expo 58. It could be argued that the design pendulum was to swing a little too far in the other direction from the criticised pre-war Paris display, but the government appears to have been sufficiently pleased with Gardner's efforts to award him a CBE. In 1935 the British had had a pavilion at the Brussels Exhibition, which was generally considered to have had an impressive exterior, but a somewhat disappointing interior display, and it was generally thought to have been a missed opportunity. Gardner was to make full use of the opportunity offered to him in 1958.

If one is to believe his own account, he virtually tackled the whole show single-handedly. He wrote 'I was given the job', and that his only briefing had been 'Get on with it G, and be sure we open on time'. The actual architecture of the Pavilion was designed by Howard V. Loeb & Partners, the Hall of Industry and the Britannic Inn were designed by Edward Mills & Partners and Gardner had Hugh Casson, and his Royal College of Art students, design

a Pavilion Garden, including such whimsy as a fountain of watering cans and mermaids under umbrellas. The Council of Industrial Design were also involved, providing a mini-Design Centre containing over two hundred exhibits, the manufacturers of which were awarded the CoID's certificate of merit.

But Gardner set the tone, and one gets the flavour of his input by his account of the entrance:

I set fly with a great cathedral-like entryhall. Deep purple, lit by a narrow shaft of light admitted through navette-shaped apertures filled with stained glass. A thick carpeted walkway flanked by heraldic banners ... To the right a sort of 'Camelot' buffet mounted with gold and silver trophies from the strong-rooms at the Tower of London ... To the left a stage half masked by the fall of a swagged drape ... On the stage a costumed group of the guys we

romantically think of as Great Men ... To terminate the 'cathedral' ... a portrait of the Queen [the controversial one by Annigoni].

Although some pageantry was to be allowed into Britain's contribution to Montreal's Expo 67, Gardner was, for this, to work with his long-term modernist associate for exhibition work, Basil Spence. This time he had a more firmly focused brief 'Britain Today' – the Central Office of Information wanted to project the contemporary scene; they must have been ill-prepared for what the maverick Gardner produced. Canada had adopted the overall theme for Expo 67 of 'Man and His World' and declared their intent as a guide to exhibiting nations:

...to demonstrate the wealth of our common knowledge and emphasise the youth of the world, the legacy of the past and the prospect of things to come.

The site was on newly built and extended islands in the St. Lawrence river, and this decision greatly helped Basil Spence in his design for the British Pavilion, his being able to symbolize Britain as a strong island state. Expo 67 was to be Spence's last exhibition work and he could be said to have gone out with a bang, for the British Pavilion stood out from the other eighty nine with its tower, emblazoned with a sculpted Union Jack (designed by F.H.K. Henrion) and its irregularly silhouetted building, surrounded on three sides by water. Spence, who like some other designers, used his exhibition work for testing out new ideas on a small scale, for Montreal had what he described as 'a

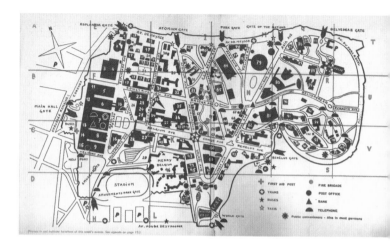

Far left: Back view of the British Pavilion, Brussels Expo 58. **Left:** The Pavilion seen across its small lake. **Above:** Map of the Brussels Expo 58.

vehicle for national propaganda' combined with 'a crucible for experimentation'.

Spence's building formed three sides of a square, the fourth being open to the water. It consisted of five separate exhibition halls linked at various levels. The shape and size of the tower was influenced by the Central Office of Information wanting to show off the Whittle jet engine, and the inside gradually morphed into one of the five themed exhibition spaces – 'Industrial Britain'. Spence's aim to produce 'a craggy, tough and uncompromising design' was likened by James Callaghan to 'the Eddystone Lighthouse seen from Plymouth Hoe'.

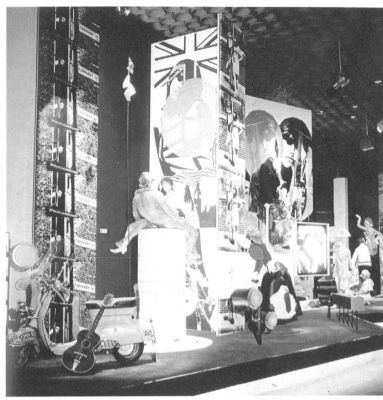

The five themes in the British Pavilion each had a different designer – Sean Kenny for 'Shaping Britain', Beverley Pick for 'The Genius of Britain', Mario Armengol for 'Britain in the World', Theo Crosby for 'Industrial Britain' and James Gardner for 'Britain Today'. It was Spence who actually chose the designers, having been associated with all five

before. Spence decreed 'no flags, no bunting, grass or flowers' and Gardner seems to have been only too eager to comply, declaring he intended to present a quirky reinterpretation of foreigners' expectations of the British. He decided to guy such stereotyping of the British as 'hypocrites, pompous asses, devious exploiters, stiff necks, stuffed shirts or just shy'; the

Far left: Mount|Evans poster for the Montreal 'Expo67'. **Left:** James Gardner's display of 60s pop culture for the British Pavilion. **Above left:** Astrid Zydower's figures for James Gardner's 'stiff-upper-lipped' family. **Above right:** Model for the British Pavilion (designer, Basil Spence, with F.H.K. Henrion's Union Jack sculpture design).

result can only, in hindsight, be described as bizarre. Gardner had a series of tableaux along the lines of a city gent with bowler hat, brief case, umbrella and 'long johns', a Hilliard miniature of an Elizabethan youth alongside a Carnaby Street 'mod', and so on.

Gardner in his rather 'schoolboy having a lark' memoires recorded:

...a local window dresser and I battled all night with slick mannequins, purchased in France ... we fixed tights to those idealized limbs with a staple-gun to the sound of the Beatles' 'Penny Lane' on tape.

Although Gardner was always up-to-date when it came to exhibition technology, including sound and film in a number of his set pieces, he appears always to have allowed a certain amount of British whimsy into his designs, as along with the Beatles and Mary Quant, he included such elements as a tea-pot playing 'Tea for Two'.

Mention must be made of Astrid Zydower's contribution to Expo67, not only because a woman's name rarely occurs in the history of exhibition design, but her figures for Gardner's tableaux, which she and her team modelled in the arches under Waterloo Station, were so striking that she was awarded an MBE. Some of these models were later auctioned for charity including a London bus 'clippy' with workable ticket machine. Gardner, who had previously worked with Zydower at the Brussel's World Fair in 1958, was to continue to commission her for similar assignments through to the 1970s.

EXHIBITION
MURALS

If it is to be regretted that most exhibition displays, however brilliant, were dismantled the moment the last visitor had left, it is even more regrettable that very few murals or backcloths to displays have survived. It is possible that most exhibition visitors would have found it difficult even to remember the content or style of most of the 'murals' they would have seen, unless they dominated an external wall, so effectively did most of them serve their purpose – creating a mood, adding meaning to a message or theme, or actually being an integral part of the story being told; 'built for purpose' most exhibition murals would tend to merge into their respective displays, providing the necessary synergy to enhance the scene.

Creating a mural or backcloth for an exhibition was a demanding commission, particularly for a 'fine' artist who might flinch at the likely ephemeral nature of the work and the fact that it was usually to show off a display rather than take centre stage,

considerations that commercial artists would be use to. In addition to such matters of 'ego', there were the actual practical challenges, not only the usual ones for commercial design of short lead times within tight budgets, but oftimes having to create onsite fitting into contractors' schedules, and, if external, coping with intemperate weather, or, if painted offsite, the problems of transporting to the site, often enormous pieces, without damage.

Murals, as such, compared to mere decorative panels in which, or against which exhibits are displayed, do not really feature large in exhibition history until after WWII. The odd early example can be found, as A.K. Lawrence's 'The Altruists' in the British Pavilion in Paris in 1925. The Glasgow Empire Exhibition of 1938 appears to be one of the first to make any marked use of murals, particularly in Misha Black's four halls in the United Kingdom Pavilion, portraying industrial resources. Each hall

Previous page: Barbara Jones's BCMI mural 'Things for Children', 1946. **Above left:** Lawrence Scarfe's mural for the British Potter Manufacturers Federation, BIF 1947 (stand designed by R.Y. Goodden). **Above right:** John R. Barker's mural for the 'Iron & Steel' Hall, UK Pavilion, Empire Exhibition Glasgow, 1938.

had a conical shaped end wall which featured these murals, the most impressive being Clive Gardiner's 'Coal', John Barker's 'Steel' and Eric Fraser's 'Fitter Britain'.

In the immediate post-war period both the 'Britain Can Make It' and the 'Enterprise Scotland' exhibitions included some murals, examples for the former being Barbara Jones' for the Children's Section, Laurence Scarfe's for the Book and Printing Section, and John Bambridge's for a kitchen display, along with one by Hans Feibusch for the exhibition

tearoom. In 'Enterprise Scotland' John Hutton, in addition to designing engraved panels, provided a mural for the wool display, which was also illustrated with one by Thomas Wales.

But it was the Festival of Britain that was to provide the opportunity for the greatest display of exhibition murals, with over one hundred murals for the main sites – backing displays and/or decorating internal or external walls. Some of the commissioned artists spent a good part of their careers as muralists, as Laurence Scarfe and Hans Feibusch, whilst for others, as Joseph Herman, Keith Vaughan, John Minton and Graham Sutherland it would have been a rare adventure.

The Festival murals ranged from the most abstract to the most realistic. Victor Pasmore, at this time making his dramatic switch from figurative to abstract, was already experimenting with organic swirls when he designed his enormous ceramic mural for the South Wall of the Regatta Restaurant. Writing of his artistic shift, Pasmore described it as 'not the result of a process of abstraction in front of nature, but a method of construction emanating from within'. His non-grouted tiles provided an overall effect of movement, albeit offending the neat standards of the tilers fixing them. Another abstract mural at the festival was that of Ben Nicholson, affixed to the entrance of the Riverside Restaurant. Nicholson seems to have been a shade precious in regards to his work, Jane Drew, the Restaurant's architect, remembering his demanding the workmen wore white gloves when handling it, and further demanded that it should be covered with glass so that the public wouldn't damage it; being curved, a glass covering would have been well outside budget.

An example of what might be described as a semi-abstract mural was John Piper's Festival mural 'The Englishman's Home', some 200ft long and made up of 42 plywood sheets, for the external wall of the Homes and Garden Pavilion. Hugh Casson had given Piper the vaguest of briefs – 'some kind of architectural congeries'. Piper, well experienced

Clive Gardiner's mural for the 'Coal Mining' Hall, UK Pavilion, Empire Exhibition, Glasgow, 1938.

Above: Edward Bawden's 'Country Life in Britain' mural for the Festival of Britain, 1951. **Right:** Eric Fraser's mural for Babcock & Wilson Ltd.

18th century architecture, with the odd suburban house wedged in, the overall colouring being altogether more subdued than upbeat. David Fraser Jenkins generously interpreted the result as implying 'Pray God, whatever it is, make sure that the new building will be as thoroughgoing as this, and as individualistic, and as prepared in due course to cede its place.'

Edward Bawden's 45ft high free-standing 'Country Life', although equally somber in colour to 'The Englishman's Home' at least, on close inspection, provides some relevant detail and light-heartedness, with the odd typical Bawden staring cow, a frisking dog, and tables showing off country produce. Bawden, under some pressure, for at the same time he was working on a mural for the Orient Line's 'Oronsay', involved a number of his former students, along with his daughter Joanna.

Graham Sutherland's 'The Origins of the Land' for the Land of Britain Pavilion, also perhaps can be placed as semi-abstract, albeit containing some clearly discernible sea life and a pterodactyl. Cadbury Brown, who designed the Pavilion, was somewhat alarmed at Sutherland's offering which Harriet Atkinson has described as 'an unsettling vision of primitive chaos in acid colours', hardly blending, she thought, with Cadbury Brown's more cosy approach to the subject. He was later to say of it:

'Hopeless … it certainly didn't work … Any rate, you walked round it, through it, past it'.

The hundred or so mural artists for the Festival

in architectural fantasies, decided to have minimal detail, but to provide a series of buildings distinguishable by their colour and their silhouettes. Piper seems to have been largely indifferent to the Festival spirit of optimism and modernism, obstinately using as his sources his personal favourites drawn from now read as a roll call of some of the major artists and designers of mid-20th century Britain including Leonard Rosoman, Keith Vaughan, John Minton, the James' – Boswell and Fitton, Felix Topolski, John Tunnard, Norman Weaver and yet to reach her public – Mary Fedden.

Relatively few commercial firms could afford to employ mural artists and consequently murals do not feature large at trade exhibitions. Some exceptions of note were Eric Fraser working for Babcock & Wilson, and Norman Weaver (trained at the Central School and working for a time with Beverley Pick) for the textile firm J.H. Birtwistle, for ICI, for Bowater and for English Electric. Two artists who merit special mention, who also made major contributions to the Festival, were Laurence Scarfe (1914–1993) and Barbara Jones (1912–1978).

Scarfe's name occurs frequently in the 1940s and

'50s as a mural artist at exhibitions. He was, in fact, a very versatile artist, and also provided illustrations for books and magazines, did some poster and advertising work, designed for wallpapers and ceramics, as well as writing and illustrating his own books. A member of the Society of Mural Painters, Scarfe designed murals for a number of buildings,

Below left: Laurence Scarfe's mural for the Regatta Restaurant at the Fesival of Britain, 1951. **Right:** A detail from Barbara Jones's mural for the International Labour Exhibition, Turin, 1961.

including the Beecham Research laboratories and The Royal Garden Hotel.

He studied painting at the Royal College of Art and provided his first exhibition mural for the British Pavilion at the Paris Exhibition of 1937. This was of a number of doll-like figures including a monkey dressed as a troubadour, in the style of the 'popular' art interests of that time. It was not until after the war that Scarfe returned to exhibition murals with his large background for the Books and Printing Section of BCMI, again with a snitch of British whimsy, a major part being taken up with a wonderfully stylized fountain, which could equally well be mistaken for a Bawden or a Ravilious; books are certainly not predominant but the whole mural, nevertheless, provides a mood of leisurely relaxation.

At the Festival of Britain his work popped up all over the place, for besides murals he designed a gift shop and a Punch & Judy Theatre for the Battersea site. He had two murals on the South Bank – one for the Regatta Restaurant, the other for the Dome of Discovery. For the Dome, Scarfe provided an image of the Nuclear Physics Laboratory at Harwell, and for the Restaurant a tryptich, for its terrace, of rowing and sailing.

Hazen Sise's mural for the Glass gallery at the RSA's 'British Art in Industry' Exhibition, 1935 (designer, Maxwell Fry).

It was during the late '40s and early '50s that Scarfe also provided murals for companies at trade shows, as the British Industries Fairs, as when he collaborated with Basil Spence for an ICI Coronation Pavilion. Most frequently mentioned in the literature, is his immense mural for BX Plastics Ltd, with stylized images of the manufacture and use of plastics.

Barbara Jones was an artist who was prepared to apply her talent to any commission that interested her, from illustrating a book cover to designing a Lord Mayor's Show, and for each she gave her own idiosyncratic interests and obsessions free rein; exhibition work being no exception. She graduated from the Royal College of Art in 1937, but it was in the post-war years that she began to design for exhibitions, much of her early work done under the direction of James Gardner. For BCMI she made a mural, a series of panels, illustrating an old nursery rhyme, completing it in some two months. A note in her archives describes the work:

A striking tableaux in the top section illustrating the famous Birthday Nursey Rhyme, from Monday's child 'fair of face' sitting before a dressing table, through the days of the week to Sunday's child 'blithe and bonny and good and gay' rightly put in a glass case out of reach of an everyday little boy who resents such perfection.

Barbara again worked with Gardner for a CoID 'Design Fair' providing three panels titled 'Nature – Man'; and some panels for a further CoID exhibition 'Enterprise Travels'. At about the same time Barbara Jones painted some ten panels for Shell to be mounted on the outside of their stands at agricultural shows, illustrating the use of Shell products for agricultural machinery. And again she worked with Gardner for the Festival of Britain, on a mural for 'The Coastline of Britain' which, in the catalogue is described as 'sampling five stretches, which are made to speak for the whole range of the island'. She also painted a mural for the Festival's Television Pavilion – a horseracing track to back a show of women's fashions. She wrote of her contributions to the Festival (working on the Pleasure Gardens as well):

I have never worked harder in my life, and most of the time it was marvellous.

Of her exhibition murals she was most proud of a head she painted on the theme 'Man at Work', for a Central Office of Information commission for an International Labour Exhibition in Turin in 1961. This found her at her most capricious for a close inspection shows that she made only the slightest attempt to adhere to the subject, (a few coal miners and farm workers), and to these she added a coffin,

Barbara Jones's mural for a Council of Industrial Design exhibition, 1948.

couples embracing, a tiger atop a crocodile, and her favourite obsession, an owl. She so treasured this work that she eventually bought it back, so it is one of the few of her mural works that is still in existence. Her one-time partner, Tom Ingram, said of her work that spontaneity was more her style than laborious effort, and although she was capable of quite meticulous work, her exhibition murals were generally fairly loosely painted and definitely eccentric in content.

EXHIBITION DESIGNERS

There was something swarm-like characterizing that brilliant generation of exhibition designers of the 1940s through to the 1960s; they tended to move en masse, in sub-swarms of a variety of combinations and permutations. To push the metaphor, the two main sourcing hives seem to have been the Camouflage Divisions of WWII, and the frantically busy Exhibition Division of the wartime Ministry of Information.

It is perhaps not surprising that camouflage work prepared artists for exhibition design, for it was to challenge their ingenuity with very limited resources in oftimes extremely short time limits, particularly relevant being the construction of dummy tanks, ships, and the like. Hulme Chadwick, James Gardner, Basil Spence, Hugh Casson, Robert Goodden, Richard Guyatt, Christopher Ironside, Richard Russell and Robin Darwin, all worked in camouflage, some working closely together, some just crossing each other's paths fleetingly.

Darwin was to be something of a queen bee, for when he began to build up his new hive at the Royal College of Art, he drew to him Casson, Goodden, Guyatt and Russell, all of whom were to work, in various combinations, on exhibitions, only Chadwick, Gardner and Spence resisting the Kensington magnet, but, in their turn, Spence and Gardner working on a number of significant exhibition commissions together.

And then there was the equally brilliant hive employed by, or associated with, the Ministry of Information during the war – Milner Gray, Misha Black, James Holland, Kenneth Bayes, Beverley Pick, Peter Moro and F.H.K. Henrion. Their 'flight', to end the metaphor, was to the Design Research Unit with Gray, Black and Bayes as its Directors. In the Ministry's case, it was to be Henrion, Holland and Pick who were to remain free agents.

Misha Black was to be the exhibition maestro, linking the two groups when he was appointed Professor at the Royal College. And a number of the Royal College group (and their wives) were also linked to exhibition design through their work for Stephen Tallents' exhibition model company, 'Cockade', including Guyatt and his wife Elizabeth Corsellis, and Casson and his wife Margaret.

To provide even brief biographies of the hundreds of designers working on exhibitions between the 1920s and 1970 would require a volume of its own. In the allotted pages herein, one criterion for short listing was those who were elected RDI with exhibition design as all, or part, of their accreditation. To these were added other RDI's who were recognized for other areas of excellence but had done exhibition design work as well; and then was added a handful of names that occurred too frequently in reportage of exhibitions as to be omitted, as, for example, architects, not eligible for RSA recognition.

There are inevitably omissions, mainly on the grounds of thinness of recorded information for the building up of a professional picture, as with V. Rotter and Robert Gutmann, or because of the limited amount of exhibition work done as compared to their other professional work, as with Kenneth Bayes, Christopher Ironside and James Holland.

Misha Black, 1910–1977

Misha Black towered above most other designers in the post-WWII years. Virtually untrained, and certainly unqualified, he went from being a youthful gofer in the East End of London rag trade to becoming Professor of Industrial Design at the Royal College of Art.

Born in Russia, he came with his family to England at the age of eighteen months; the family changed its name from the Russian Tcherny, to its English equivalent 'Black'. Little is known of his schooling except for a reminiscence in the RCA's student magazine 'Ark'. In this he wrote that art was the only subject for which he showed any aptitude and that from an early age he aspired to be an artist (and he implied 'commercial') as the best means he had of 'avoiding malnutrition'.

However, in order not to starve on leaving school, he had to make do with odd jobs in the rag and furniture trades, with some evening classes at the Central School. Yet such was his motivation that by seventeen, in 1928, he had found work designing posters, through the agency J. Arundell-Clarke; and, at much the same time, he got his first exhibition commission – a stand for the Rio Tinto Company at the Seville Exhibition. This opened the door to more exhibition work for a wide range of goods and services – from food (for such companies as Cerebos, Toblerone, and Crosse & Blackwell), to technical products (for the Standard Motor Company, Esso and Kelvinator).

For a brief period of about a year he worked in partnership with Lucy Rossetti, as Studio Z, taking on any work that came to hand, including exhibitions. On her becoming ill, Black began to work on his own until 1933 when he joined Bassett-Gray, which Milner Gray had founded with some of his Goldsmith College friends in 1922. Black continued to work with them when they were reformed as the Industrial Design Partnership, through to 1940. At IDP Black continued with exhibition work, but began to develop a reputation for product design. Little of this early exhibition work is specifically recorded apart from what was referred to as 'an ingenious portable exhibition stand' in *Shelf Appeal* – 'Shepherds, farmers and 'The County' fell for Misha Black's new portable exhibit'.

It was about this time that Black began to write articles for the press, particularly for *Shelf Appeal*, on design work generally, including exhibitions. Even in this pre-war period he was envisaging the possibility of using narratives, particularly if there was an educational or propaganda element to an exhibition. The most notable of Black's pre-war exhibition work was for the MARS group, for which he became secretary, in spite of lacking the professional qualifications of most of its members – architects and engineers. He replaced Moholy Nagy as the designer for the

Misha Black's work for the 'Darkness into Daylight' exhibition at the Science Museum, 1948 (with Bronek Katz, Norman Frith, Ronald Sandiford and John Barker.

MARS Exhibition of 1938 – 'New Architecture' – for which his contribution was rated as 'heralding a new approach to exhibition design'. Other pre-war exhibitions to which he contributed were several halls for the UK Pavilion at the Empire Exhibition in 1938, and for the halls in the British Pavilion at the New York 'World's Fair' in 1939.

All of this made Black a much sought after designer for Milner Gray to have in his team in the wartime Exhibition Division of the Ministry of Information; but there was a snag, for Black was still Russian and, as such, was barred from the Civil Service. Gray got round this by getting him employed as a consultant on a weekly basis, albeit he is usually described as Principal Exhibition Architect to the Ministry. At the end of the war, from 1945 onwards, Black was to work along with Gray as Directors of the newly formed Design Research Unit; and from 1959 through to 1977 he held the post of Professor of Industrial Design at the RCA.

Black's first major post-war exhibition design was when the Council of Industrial Design gave him the key task of demonstrating the design process at its 'Britain Can Make It' exhibition in 1946; his 'The Birth of an Egg Cup' got a rather mixed reception. Black, an enthusiast of the 1851 Great Exhibition, then conceived a plan for a centenary exhibition, but this was overtaken by the Atlee government's plan for the Festival of Britain. Black was brought into the Festival's Presentation Panel and given responsibility as coordinating architect of the South Bank Upstream section, which included coordinating displays for the Dome of Discovery, and being co-architect for the Regatta Restaurant and the Bailey Bridge.

In recording his contribution to the Festival, Black wrote that his objectives had been aesthetic – to demonstrate the quality of modern architecture and town planning; and to show that painters and sculptors could work along with architects, landscape architects and exhibition designers to produce an 'aesthetic unity'. Although he claimed success on both counts, he rather shot himself in the foot by later writing that there had been 'little real innovation'.

That exhibition design had been an important element in his work, even before the Festival, is evidenced in that he edited and contributed to what he claimed was the first textbook on the subject (not true given Weaver's tome of 1923). In 'Exhibition Design' Black not only got together some of the leading exponents in the field, as Spence, Holland, Guyatt and Goslett, but he, himself, wrote a comprehensive introductory overview, defining the role of an exhibition designer and providing a simple classification of exhibitions.

After the Festival, Black became increasingly focused on commercial interior design, product design and corporate image programmes, the last with his extensive work for British Rail, and acting as design consultant for London Transport. And he was increasingly international in assignments. Avril Blake lists his activities in one year, 1956, taking him to Paris, Toronto, Vienna, Montreal, Budapest and Canada. Much of this was consultancy or chairing conferences but also some exhibition design as for the UK Pavilion at the Rhodes Centenary Exhibition, the British Exhibition at the Tenth Trienniale in Milan, and the odd stand for a British Industries Fair.

Blake, summing up Black's career, wrote 'It had been a long way from Cinderella and he had had to be his own Prince Charming' – from an East End runner Black built himself into an international design guru, receiving a multitude of accolades – RDI in 1957, President of the DIA, Professor Emeritus of RCA, and a knighthood in 1972. The range of his achievements was honoured posthumously with the establishment, in 1978, of the Sir Misha Black Medal, awarded for international contribution to design education, and, in 1999, by the Sir Misha Black Award for innovation in Design Education for UK educationalists.

Stefan Buzas, 1915–2008

When Stefan Buzas was asked to choose three of his designs that he considered best represented his work, on being made an RDI in 1961, he included his design for 'The Land' in the Dome of Discovery for the Festival of Britain, along with his Waterford Glass showroom (1972) and his Treasury for Chichester Cathedral (1975). Most of his career was concerned with buildings and their interiors, (most notably for travel firms in Piccadilly and Manchester Airport); but, for a short period in the 1940s and early '50s his name frequently had 'exhibition design' attached to it.

Buzas was born in Hungary, but started his architectural training at the Technische Hochschule in Vienna. For safety, being Jewish, his parents sent him to England in 1938, where he finished his professional training at the Architectural

Above: Stefan Buzas's display for Lewis Berger and Sons Ltd., *c*.1949. **Far right:** Hugh Casson's UK Pavilion at the Van Riebeeck Festival Fair, Cape Town, 1952.

Association (AA). Soon after completing his course Buzas started teaching in the architectural department at Kingston School of Art. It was here that he met Eric Brown, with whom he was to design for a number of exhibitions in the immediate post-war years – 'The Wallpaper Exhibition' (1945), 'The Londoner's England' exhibition at Charing Cross Underground Station (1946), some diplays for the Arts Council (1946) and the 'Story of Wool' (1947), again at Charing Cross.

By 1948, with colleagues from the AA, he set up James Cubitt & Partners. The concern expanded, possibly too quickly, with offices overseas, and subsequently the partnership began to break up, Buzas eventually leaving in 1965 when he opened an office with Alan Irvine. A few exhibitions bear Buzas's name, working alone (neither with Brown, nor his partners) as in 1949, for the exhibition 'Darkness into Light' and for Lewis Berger paints at the Motor show; and in 1951, a stand for the Zinc Development Corporation at the Building Trades Exhibition.

As so many other architects, he was drawn into designing for the Festival of Britain – a section on earth sciences in the Dome of Discovery; some odd references actually attach his name to that of Ralph Tubbs, accrediting both with the Dome's design. Irvine described Buzas's section as 'an oasis of order and clarity in the confusion of that interior'. The Festival seems to have been Buzas's last major contribution to exhibition design for after that he seems to have been content to run a modest office, and, with Irvine, to have concentrated on buildings' interiors.

Hugh Casson, 1910–1999

It came as something of a surprise to some that Hugh Casson was appointed Director of Architecture for the Festival of Britain for he had had a relatively limited experience of exhibition design, certainly when compared to those working for the Ministry of Information during the war. Nevertheless he was to prove himself effective in the post, both for his imaginative ideas and his handling of people.

Casson had been brought up by grandparents in Kent, his father working in India. He had enjoyed his art classes at Eastbourne College, but was persuaded, against his inclination, not to pursue an artistic career, but to apply to Cambridge to read Classics. It was only when he got himself to the Cambridge School of Architecture, in 1929, that Casson found his true métier.

It was at Cambridge he met Christopher Nicholson, who was to become his future business partner. The two of them, as officers in the University's Architectural Society, were to arrange for a number of notable speakers, and from this, Casson was to build up a considerable network of useful contacts. A relative, Lewis Casson, married to the actress Sybil Thorndike, was another useful link for work he was later to do for the theatre.

Casson combined a natural talent for sketching out ideas with an easy writing style, and after a period at the Bartlett School of Architecture in London he began to write and illustrate articles for the architectural press. In the partnership with Nicholson he was very much the front man. The first exhibition that they worked on together was for the MARS group. The partnership split up during the war, with Nicholson going into the Fleet Air Arm and Casson working in camouflage and then in the Ministry of Town & Country Planning. The partnership was renewed at the end of the war and the odd exhibition commission came their way. Casson was attracted to display as it tended to require speed of ideas and a degree of theatricality which he had found satisfying in the stage work he had done via Lewis Casson; an example of his attraction to 'drama' was his description of a stand he did for Berketex as 'a fibrous rendering of Strawberry Hill Gothic'.

When Barry offered him the Festival of Britain challenge he was possibly as bewildered as others:

...I signed up on this 1951 job on one condition that either I was given a considerable amount of designing to do within the 1951, or if the job was largely 'ideas' I should be given the opportunity of doing work OUTSIDE the job.

Casson found himself fully employed! Morrison's instructions to Casson were – 'I don't want to know how it's going. Just get on with it, and come back if you're in real trouble.'

Although he said he didn't want to be an ideas man, and, indeed he immediately demonstrated his social skill in getting the various design teams into place, Richard Guyatt was to say that he was, in fact, 'an absolute sparkle, fizzing away like a rocket'. He was reported as having most of the bright ideas, and made quick conceptual sketches of all the envisaged buildings.

If Casson hadn't particularly distinguished himself as an exhibition designer prior to the Festival, his handling of the enormous task, not only brought him a knighthood, but the confidence to take on bigger architectural challenges than before. Along with his long term business partner, Neville Conder, he is best remembered for the Elephant House at the London Zoo, and a long term development for Cambridge University.

Much of Casson's post-Festival work could be described as 'interior' and decorative, as for the Royal Yacht Club and for Glynbourne, exhibitions, as such, were rare; indeed he was titled Professor of Interior Design when he worked at the Royal College of Art from 1955 to 1975. His writing, lecturing, broadcasting and television added to his becoming one of the most popular figures in the arts; in 1976 he was elected President of the Royal Academy, a position he held through to 1984. The Festival of Britain may have been his main contribution to exhibition design, but it brought him a knighthood (he was to become a Companion of Honour in 1985); and, looking back, he seems to have derived much personal satisfaction that, in his own words, his contribution had 'made people want things to be better and to believe they could be'.

Hulme Chadwick, 1910–1977

... a high-domed forehead, an alarming piercing eye, a red Kaiser moustache, a North Country accent, forthright speech, and a bluff, cheerful, casual manner that concealed ... a complex and sensitive personality. Hugh Casson

Hulme Chadwick is a name known to few these days, but in his hey day, from the 1940s through to the '60s, he was considered one of a handful of elite designers for exhibitions; certainly he was one of the most prolific. In all he was to work for over eighty projects, either designing individual stands or acting as exhibition architect. It was to Chadwick that the Royal Society of Arts turned to design their own 'Exhibition of Exhibitions', the Society's contribution to the Festival of Britain.

View of the 'Exhibition of Exhibitions', Royal Society of the Arts, 1951, Hulme Chadwick.

Chadwick was born and brought up in Manchester. He left school at the age of fourteen and found work in the design office of a local cotton mill, attending art classes in the evening. In 1929 he won an Industrial Art Exhibition Scholarship enabling him to study on a full-time basis at the Manchester College of Art. A year later he won a national scholarship to the Royal College of Art where he graduated in 1934, being awarded a travelling scholarship.

WWII was to interrupt his budding career as a designer; he joined the camouflage division of the

Air Ministry, rising to become its Chief Camouflage Officer. At the end of the war he started up his own practice, eventually named Hulme Chadwick & Partners, when he took on Allen Boothroyd and Roy Walker and brought in his two sons – Andrew, a qualified architect, and Fergus, as the practice's business administrator.

Chadwick was a versatile designer, putting his hand to an enormous number of diverse projects, from designing the interior of an aircraft for BOAC, working on shop interiors, as for Liberty's, turning to hotel interiors for British Transport Hotels; and then spreading his talents for a total corporate identity programme for Bass Charrington, as well as dabbling in product design for Wilkinson Sword (for which he won a number of Council of Industrial Design awards).

And along with all this, he was no slouch when it came to his commitment to his professionalism, for at the age of 45 he sat for the examinations of the Royal Institute of British Architects! In 1952 he was made a Fellow of the Society of Industrial Artists and Designers, and in 1966, its President; in 1956 he became a Fellow of RIBA, and in 1975 was elected RDI.

As early as 1947, *Art & Industry* devoted an article to his work, which started 'A specialist with an enviable reputation for versatility', and which particularly commended his '...lack of personal style, his ability to bend his talents to the specific challenge in hand'. Chadwick was featured again in the journal in 1949 for his work for Lilley & Skinner's shoe shop in Oxford Street; whilst in 1953, a whole article was devoted to his design of exhibition stands for ICI.

ICI was to be one of Chadwick's major clients when it came to exhibition design. In the eight years between 1952 and 1960 he is thought to have designed some twenty one stands for the various divisions of the company, both for UK and overseas exhibitions, in such locations as Montreal, New York, Zurich, Stockholm and Johannesburg. One of his most striking stands was that for the British Industries Fair in 1953 when his challenge was to publicise ICI's new products Ardil and Terylene in the Central Hall at Earls Court, and to persuade haute couture designers to run up sufficient models for gracing his stand, which was dominated by ceiling high pylons draped with fabric.

Chadwick designed stands for many other companies including Sandersons, Mullards Radios, Shell, British Aluminium and Smith's Clocks, not infrequently designing for more than one company at the same exhibition. Between 1956 and 1960 he designed some ten stands for the United Kingdom Atomic Energy Authority, and for some four years for Shell for Eastern European shows. For the Festival of Britain he not only designed the RSA exhibition, but the Exhibition of Books at the V&A, and for the Heavy Engineering Exhibition in Glasgow.

Hulme Chadwick's display stand for the National Coal Board, *c.*1949.

Although, as *Art & Industry* said, he was willing to adapt to the variety of the commissions he undertook, Chadwick was very much his own man. Not only was he an excellent designer, but he had a thorough understanding of contractors and was a determined negotiator. For each commission he would demand a solid time allowance for prior research and discussion and for gestation. He had a solid confidence in his own competence, once declaring 'I must be right or I'm useless'. And after the prior planning he insisted on working independently – 'any attempt to interfere after commencement of operations will be strongly challenged'.

Although Chadwick stressed the need for all parties involved in an assignment to be in agreement, his own ability to compromise was tempered by his self-confidence in his design concepts, and in his ability to see a project through, on time and within budget – a truly effective commercial designer.

Cockade

Cockade, a model designing and making company was the brain child of Stephen Tallents, described by his admirers as 'an imaginative civil servant', or by his detractors as something of a maverick. Tallents was an extraordinary personality with an extraordinary career – before WW1 he helped

Front cover of Cockade publicity portolio.

public relations with his booklet 'The Projection of England'; he became the first President of the Institute of Public Relations. How then did he come to run an exhibition model-making business in South Kensington?

During and after the war his meteoric career had begun to falter, and, frustrated by life at the BBC, where he was its first Controller of Public Relations and the Ministry of Town & Country Planning, he left and decided to set up his own small enterprise where he could use his initiative without the constraints of operating within the civil service. Tallents was quite a practical man; there is report of him skinning animals on his country estate and using the skins for binding books, a service he tried to sell to the various libraries and museums! During his time at the Ministry of Town and Country Planning he had networked with architects and designers including Hugh Casson and Richard Guyatt and, by 1946, he had Guyatt on Cockade's board of directors, along with Peter Barker-Mill, an artist and patron of the arts.

In a Cockade publicity leaflet, published in 1949, Tallents wrote that he had already appreciated, whilst at the EMB, that people learn more from 'visuals' than from reading texts. In particular he had discerned a market gap for better designed 'visuals' – models for window and architectural displays:

I was rarely satisfied by the design, the colouring, the craftsmanship and the setting of the models I saw publicly displayed.

Beveridge establish labour exchanges; at the end of the war for a short time he was virtually the ruler of three Baltic states; in the 1920s and into the '30s he was responsible for the ground breaking publicity of the Empire Marketing Board (EMB), and in the 1930s, along with his young protégée, virtually gave birth to British documentary film making; he brought publicity energy to the Post Office and could be said to have generally pioneered government

EDUCATIONAL DISPLAYS

Two of a series of six displays designed by CHRISTOPHER IRONSIDE and ELIZABETH CORSELLIS for MISHA BLACK. (E.L.M.A. 'Darkness Into Daylight' Exhibition, Science Museum, 1948) *Dimensions*: 3 ft. ×3 ft.

Sample page from the Cockade Portfolio, showing work by Christopher Ironside and Elizabeth Corsellis, 1948.

He had started a documentary film unit with few resources, why couldn't he make a similar start in this area. He began to build up a team of skilled employees along with a number of 'associates'; he found premises in South Kensington, along with a workshop; he began to advertise his services:

The designing and execution of exhibitions, individual exhibition and showroom displays, shop window displays and travelling exhibitions.

His production manager, T.W. Hendrick, was later to record:

Here, under one roof, was gathered all the essential creative talent and skill necessary for the entire production of exhibits and displays.

Tallents not only involved Casson and Guyatt, but their wives, Margaret Casson and Elizabeth Corsellis, and the list of designers and exhibiting companies and organization making use of Cockade's team began to grow. Amongst major designers, Misha Black and James Gardner were to use Cockade for a variety of commissions, with Black occasionally doing assignments for Cockade himself. The company's clients were spread widely across industries, but perhaps the one giving them best validity was the Council of Industrial Design. Amongst the projects Cockade carried out for the Council were models, designed by Guyatt, for a Council stand showing the design process, at the British Industries Fair in 1947; a relief, designed by Christopher Ironside, for CoID's 'Design Fair'; and display boxes for the Council's work in schools.

Cockade contributed to a number of exhibition stands, for both the British Industries Fairs and Ideal Home Exhibitions of the late 1940s. A report on a stand they produced for Sanderson's wallpapers and fabrics for the 1948 Ideal Home Exhibition gives a brief idea of their modus operandi – first making a half final scale model and then, when this was approved, making scale working drawings for the workshop for construction. At this time Guyatt, Casson and Corsellis were working for Cockade, in different combinations, as for the 'Three Hundred

126

Opposite: Travelling exhibition displays, designed by Robert Wetmore (Cockade) for CoID.
Above: Richard Guyatt's Cockade exhibition stand for Wedgwood, BIF 1949.

Years of Catering' exhibition held at the Tea Centre.

But Cockade's finest hour was probably its work for the Festival of Britain. Scott Anthony, Tallents's biographer, considered that he 'exerted a considerable influence on the presentation of the Festival, from the margins', describing this influence as 'all-persuasive'. This 'influence' is fairly fully recounted in Hendrick's section in *A Tonic for the Nation* – how Cockade's services were employed in most of the Festival's Pavilions on the South Bank; how, at the same time,

Cockade was working on seven large exhibitions stands on three different sites for the BIF; how, at the South Bank, the rain leaked through to their expensive model of the projected BBC television set-up; how his sleep over the lead-up period to the Festival opening consisted of naps on the train to Birmingham, and his watching the dawn break over the Thames after many a night's work. Cockade's contribution was not just a matter of design and construction but of a good deal of prior research – the

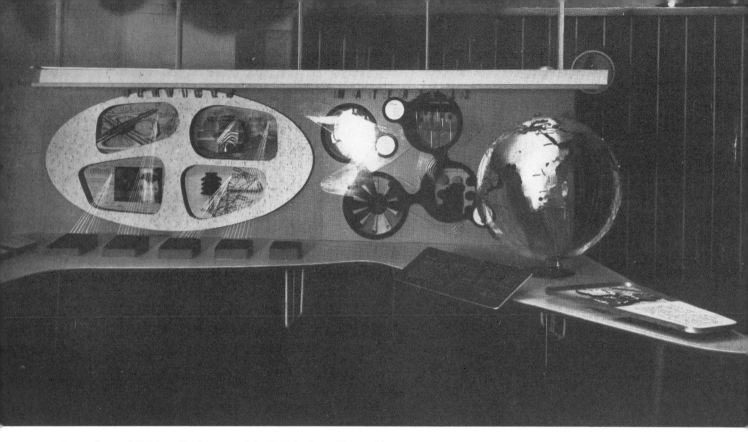

Part of an exhibition display stand for ICI designed by Robin Day, *c.*1949.

telescopes of the great astronomers, the history of the whaling industry, the TV mast at Sutton Coldfield, the Magna Carta, and so on. Of particular note was Cockade's recreation of the opening of the Great Exhibition of 1851, which included forty six little figurines of the royal family, court and government, along with a scale model of the Crystal Palace. The

reader can catch from the tone of Hendrick's description the exhilaration of Cockade's team 'putting their entire energies into the task'.

With its work not only for exhibitions and the Festival, but for many architectural projects, Cockade can be rated one of the leading display consultancies in the post-war years.

Robin Day, 1915–2010

Robin Day is best remembered as a furniture designer, particularly for his work with S. Hille and Co. Ltd. through the 1950s and '60s, a number of his designs winning the Council of Industrial Design (later the Design Council) Annual Awards. And it was Day who furnished Peter Moro's Festival Hall interiors with chairs that were to survive for some fifty years. It is altogether less well known that Day had a considerable reputation as an exhibition designer and that he continued designing for exhibitions from 1946, through to the 1970s.

Day was born in the furniture making area of High Wycombe. After a period at a technical school he went on to the local art school and from there into the drawing office of a local furniture factory. Whilst working he continued with classes at High Wycombe School of Art which enabled him to gain a scholarship to the Royal College of Art, where, because of the limited syllabus on offer, he was deflected to studying mural painting, publicity design, display and interior design.

Asthma kept Day out of the Services in WWII, during which he made what living he could with odd assignments, and by teaching, on a part-time basis, at Croydon and Beckenham Schools of Art. It was when he started to teach interior design at Regent Street Polytechnic in 1945 that his fortunes changed, for he met up with a fellow teacher, Peter Moro, an architect, who had worked on exhibitions for the Ministry of Information during the war. Moro began to involve Day in exhibition commissions, the idea being that Moro, the more experienced, should work on the general layout, and Day, with his specialist training, should detail the display and its graphics.

Their first major collaboration – 'Jet' – mounted in Charing Cross Underground Station for the Central Office of Information in 1946, on the development of new technologies for the aviation industry, had an immediate impact, and has become something of an icon in the history of exhibition design. A description by Lesley Jackson gives some idea of how striking it must have been to the visitor:

At the entrance the visitors were confronted with a revolving impellor [the heart of a gas turbine], framed dramatically within a stream-lined cross-section of a jet engine, with sweeping arrows indicating air-flow. Within the main display a series of jet airplane models suspended from the ceiling indicated the direction of visitor circulation, while photographs of actual planes in flight formed a dynamic high level frieze. The evocative whine of jet engines was relayed at intervals and diagrams were used extensively, with bubbles of text elucidating key facts.

Day provided a striking poster for 'Jet' – his first poster – which so impressed the authorities that he was subsequently commissioned to do a series for RAF and WAAF recruitment. 'Jet' led to further exhibitions for CoI as 'British Scientific Instruments – Precisely Yours', again at Charing Cross; and a stand for the General Post Office at Radiolympia 1947, explaining to the public the considerable range of the GPO's activities. The pair designed a further exhibition in 1947, this time for the Atomic Energy Authority, which was mounted in two railway coaches to tour the country. A third exhibition, in the same year, was for the National Coal Board – 'The Miner Comes to Town'.

All of these, and other minor ones, crammed together in the immediate post-war years, gave Day the experience and confidence to go it alone, particularly as Moro became increasingly involved in architectural projects. As early as 1946 Day had begun to take commissions from ICI, and for the following fifteen years or so he was to provide exhibition stands for both the ICI Group and for several of its divisions, particularly to explain new plastics when they arrived on the scene, for which his early essays in translating complex scientific and technical matters for public understanding would have stood him in good stead.

Day also had a relationship of some dozen years, from 1949 to 1961, with EKCO, the makers of bakelite radios. Jackson, in his appreciation of Day's specific design qualities that differentiated his stands from others, writes of his minute attention to detail, his sleek rectilinearity, and his controlled architectural quality.

Day, who had virtually taught himself typography, fuelled by his own enthusiasm, worked along with Milner Gray on the signage for the Festival of Britain. And he was further involved in the Festival, contributing to the Home Entertainment section of the Homes & Gardens Pavilion. Gray described their partnership at the Festival as 'successful and companionable'. Soon after the Festival, Gray, the arch exponent of exhibition design, wrote an article evaluating Day's career to that date. Gray stressed that by choosing to work alone, Day, of necessity, acquired the skills usually provided by a design team, of planning, structural design, lighting, two-dimensional display and typography. Gray particularly admired what he described as Day's 'keen sense of formal values' allied to his 'preference for contemporary idiom' which led to Day's exhibition design so effectively achieving its ends.

Although Day became increasingly taken up with furniture, carpet and interior design, he continued with his exhibition work for EKCO and ICI, along with stands for Hille and Grays Carpets. And it was for exhibition as well as furniture design that Day was made an RDI in 1959; he was to receive an OBE in 1983. In 2001 Lesley Jackson curated a major exhibition on the work of Day and his wife, Lucienne; and a retrospective for the pair was held in 2010 at Pallant House, Chichester, near to where they lived. The press release for this made no mention of his years of exhibition design, and again this was generally missed out of Day's obituaries, apart from that of Lesley Jackson. Yet it was for exhibition design that Day had been best able to demonstrate the considerable range of his talents and abilities in coordinated design, not infrequently, especially in his work with Hille, showing off his own product designs at the same time.

The Design Research Unit

A few names occur quite frequently in the design press in relation to exhibitions, along with illustrations of their work, but bare mention in the text, as, for example, Austin Frazer and Robert Gutmann; other names, better known for other design activities, also have illustrations of their exhibition work featured in journals, but again, with but scant mention of their being commissioned for such, as Kenneth Bayes and Bronek Katz. The reason for such omissions is that they were working either as part of a team, or associated with a team – the Design Research Unit (DRU). In their book on the Unit, John and Avril Blake entitle the group of designers who so gathered together – 'Practical Idealists'. Their 'Ideal' was to build a comprehensive design consultancy – 'a service to advise on all problems of design'.

The history of DRU has been well covered by books and articles; suffice it to say here that from its numerous design commissions over the years, since it was founded in 1943, from graphics and products to buildings and total corporate identity programmes, its work for exhibitions seems to have been most concentrated in the 1950s. It is not always easy to discern who did what, in relation to DRU's exhibition work, as the designers worked together in myriads

Design Research Unit's stand for *The Farmers Weekly*, credited to the work of Alexander Gibson, Austin Frazer and Misha Black as consultant.

of combinations and permutations, some fully paid employees of the Unit, some merely associates, some named, but it not being always specified what their contribution had been; very frequently the designs were just attributed to the generic term 'DRU' without individual designers being named at all.

To exemplify the problem for researchers, Volume II of Designers in Britain, published in 1951, has Misha Black along with Norman Frith working on the 'Darkness into Light' exhibition, along with Austin Frazer on a UNESCO touring exhibition, working with Austin Frazer and Brian Peake for stands for the Petroleum Information Bureau and for the Milk Marketing Board; whilst Austin Frazer

131

paired up with Stirling Craig on a stand for Shell
Chemicals and with Misha Black and Alexander
Gibson on a stand for *Farmers' Weekly*. And, at
much the same time, Frazer was working with
Robert Gutmann on a travelling exhibition 'Bringing
up Baby' and Gutmann, in turn, was alongside
G. Hoffstead on a commission for the Anglo-Iranian
Oil Company! The Blakes wrote that:

*...it was essentially a group operation among
friends in which each job was discussed on the
basis of equality amongst everyone concerned and
the work carried out by whoever was thought best
qualified to tackle it.*

Kenneth Bayes who had worked with Black
and Gray before WWII in the Industrial Design
Partnership, would tend to get involved if a commission had architectural aspects; Austin Frazer seems
to have been used for general display work, but also
to have been a DRU typographical specialist, and so
on. Usually, if Misha Black was involved, he would be
accredited as coordinating designer. Certainly this
was so for the 'Britain Can Make It' exhibition, for
the section 'What Industrial Design Means', when
he had, as his support team, Bronek Katz, Austin
Frazer and R. Vaughan. It was Milner Gray who
was to act as Designer in Chief for the exhibition of
RDI's designers – 'Design at Work' when he not only
led DRU employees and associates but had on board

James Gardner, an independent. For the Festival of
Britain, there were yet further combinations, when
Alexander Gibson worked with Black on the Regatta
Restaurant and the Bailey Bridge, Bayes had a team
of nine working with him in the Dome of Discovery,
Milner Gray and his team designed signing, and
Brian Peake was appointed the co-ordinating archi-
tect and designer of the Science Exhibition.

The Blakes chose to use DRU as the focus for their
book on post-war British design history because of
its key role:

*It is probably the oldest, largest, and best known
industrial design office in Europe; the people
responsible for its growth have made, as individuals,
profound contributions to the ideas which have
enabled industrial design to be accepted throughout
the world...*

Although DRU continued to do some exhibition
work after the Festival, its interests began to broad-
en to include more architectural assignments and
large corporate identity programmes, as for British
Rail. In relation to exhibition design, DRU, a 'group
of friends', was certainly one of the most prolific and
influential teams working in exhibition design in the
early post-war years.

Joseph Emberton, 1889–1956

It is indispensable that an exhibition is best when
conceived as a whole, for under these circumstances
it is more likely to present to the visitor a spectacle

133

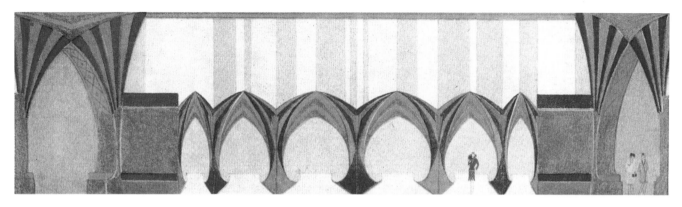

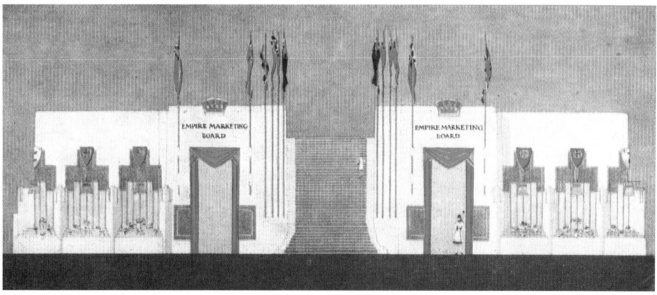

Exhibition stands designed by Joseph Emberton for the Avertising Exhibition of 1927. **Top:** plans for the 'Palace of Beauty'. **Above:** Plans for the Empire Marketing Board stand.

which influences him, evoking his admiration and holding his interest from the beginning. As a result the visitor feels that the exhibition is one, every bit of which is worth seeing and consequently the success of the individual stall-holder is assured.

Joseph Emberton is best remembered as the 'modernist' architect for Simpson's of Piccadilly and for the Royal Corinthian Yacht Club at Burnham-on-Crouch. Growing up in Blackpool, I think of him in relation to his designs for the Pleasure Beach, a swan song for him, but a delight for us youngsters. Little is remembered of his exhibition designs – yet he was one of the most progressive in this field from the 1920s onwards, and, in fact, designed one of exhibitions' main venues – the New Empire Hall at Olympia.

Born on the edge of the Potteries, Emberton was initially articled to local architects, cycling to the Burslem Art School for evening classes. Winning a scholarship to what was then the Kensington College of Art (the RCA) he found his course totally uninspiring being traditional in character, but, nevertheless, graduated with a Certificate in Architecture in 1913.

On leaving College, Pemberton joined Trehearne & Norman, then developing the ponderous large buildings along Kingsway in London. It was at this time he met Thomas Tait and John Burnett, whose practice was also working on projects around Kingsway, but whose ideas were anything but 'uninspiring' or 'ponderous', but rather influenced by what was going on internationally in architectural design.

After serving in the honourable Artillery Company in WWI, Emberton firstly worked with John Burnett, but, by 1922, had joined Percy Westwood, who specialized in retail and exhibition design. Emberton worked on some minor exhibition stands before the pair were given a major commission for the British Empire Exhibition of 1924–5. Some of the pair's assignments for the Exhibitions are credited to them both, as for the State Express Pavilion, but for others, Emberton seems to have worked alone. Inde implies that the series of 'kiosks' for commercial firms, running alongside the lake and down the main avenue were Emberton's but Weaver's account of them links Emberton with Westwood as the designers. *Commercial Art* described them as 'posters in three dimensions', for each kiosk was shaped to echo the actual packaging of the particular company's product. Emberton's contributions to the Exhibition certainly clashed with the more traditional offerings; he declared himself totally against the taste at the time of 'antique mahogany and walnut'. He later was to write that 'the conflicting ideas of many various designers have been the failing of exhibitions in the past', possibly with the Empire Exhibition in mind.

Even more 'modernist' were Emberton's design for stands for the various Advertising Exhibitions that started in the 1920s. *Commercial Art* featured three of his stands – for the Empire Marketing Board, British Railways and for the Palace of Beauty for the Advertising Exhibition of 1927. These actually have a certain 'Egyptian' touch, which could as well be linked to the stir caused by Howard Carter's excavations as by Rosemary Ind's linking the style to Emberton's war service in Egypt. Yet even more excitingly art deco were Emberton's stands for the 1933 Advertising Exhibition, with their sleek white exteriors and rounded ends, some of which are credited to him alone, but one, for Pritchard, Wood & Partners, has him as collaborating with John Gloag, the writer on design and architecture.

Although the bulk of Emberton's later output was architectural there was a combining of this with exhibitions in his 1929 New Empire Hall and his striking Soleil Pavilion for the Paris Exhibition of 1937. As early as 1928 *Commercial Art* was recognizing him as 'one of the ablest and most versatile of our young architects', and, specifically, about his contribution to the Advertising Exhibitions, considered that 'his progressive outlook and compelling initiative must exercise a healthy influence'. His 'influence' if he had such, was certainly from his permanent structures; but it could be argued that the controversy about the balance of central control for exhibition design versus individuality (possibly eccentricity) had started with Emberton's Empire Exhibition designs and his ideas on the subject, an issue that was to continue to be a concern for exhibition designers, throughout the 20th century, with the pendulum swinging first one way then the other, whenever an exhibition was to be mounted.

James Gardner, 1907–1995

When I gravitated to designing exhibitions I found I was at an advantage. Clients would argue or 'correct' scripts but the visual aspect was rarely questioned, so I had the objective world to play with by myself and to this extent was in control of the situation, just as I had been when playing with bricks as a child.

Gardner is something of an enigma. If one would judge him solely by his own writings about his activities and the record of his career he supplied to the Royal Society of Arts on becoming an RDI, he would come across as a brash, confident extrovert, charging around, tackling commissions virtually single-handedly. For example on his contribution to the 'Britain Can Make It' exhibition he claimed to have designed the layout, selected the designers, hired the contractors and worked at it sixteen hours a day. Basil Spence, its Chief Architect barely gets a look in. And for the British contribution to the Brussels World Fair he records being briefed 'Get on with it G, and be sure we open on time' – a small being, given this particular box of bricks to play with as he would. He once claimed to have designed in a larger field 'than any man living'.

Yet there is a note in the Royal Society of Arts file on James Gardner that he had little interest in self-promotion. And Hugh Casson in his obituary on Gardner described him as a quiet family man, shunning the limelight, and, in his work, relating modestly to his cooperating designers and

James Gardner's Piazza design at the Battersea site, Festival of Britain, 1951.

craftsman. This seems to be supported by Gardner listing at the back of his book *The ARTful Designer*, 'a few of the hundreds of creative artists and craftsmen who dedicated a slice of their lives to converting my visuals to a reality'. It is possible that the 'true' Gardner lies somewhere in between – an informal man, without fuss or temperament, yet with an extraordinary confidence that enabled him to take on the most challenging assignments, often under difficult conditions.

Gardner trained at Westminster School of Art. His first job was as a jewelry designer at Cartier, after which he joined the Carlton Studios, where he was expected to take on any commission coming in. It was while he was at Carlton that he got his first exhibition job from Jack Beddington of Shell-Mex

BP. This was to design an exhibition on aviation, demonstrating the use of the Company's products. There was to be no more exhibition work until after the war, in which Gardner served in Camouflage. This actually provided him with the most excellent groundwork as it involved technical drawing, graphic design, model making, photography and ingenuity – all of which are essential to exhibition design. It is recorded that 'he was a key element in the Allies' D-Day deception invasion plans'.

Gardner's first major exhibition, which is suggested he got through Beddington, was for the Council of Industrial Design's 'Britain Can Make It' in 1946. This was to be followed by dozens of other exhibition commissions, from major assignments as for the Festival of Britain (for which he was Chief Designer for the Pleasure Gardens at Battersea and for the "People of Britain'), 'Enterprise Scotland' (1947), the British Pavilion at the Brussels World Fair (1958), the British Exhibition in New York for the Board of Trade (1960), and the British Pavilion in Montreal's 'Expo67'; to more domestic shows as the Ideal Home Exhibition (intermittently throughout the 1950s into the 60s), the British Industries Fairs, and a number of small 'specialist' exhibitions as 'Atoms for Peace' (1955).

Gardner was also to become a major designer for museum displays and saw no difference between this and his exhibition work; he was to build a distinguished international reputation for both. That he had the versatility to visually narrate so many different topics was due to the fact that although art school trained, he had strong interests in technical and scientific fields – he had a glider pilot's licence, wrote children's books on flying, had contributed to the design of a plane, and was to be the first artist to be given free rein to design a ship 'above the waterline' (QE2). And these interests were perfectly combined with an ingenious imagination (for one exhibition he built a cow from a football bladder and bagpipes) – he described himself as a 'self-made cobbler up of things'.

Gardner's major contribution, to exhibition and museum design, was acknowledged by his becoming an RDI (Exhibitions) in 1947, a CBE in 1958, a Fellow of the Royal College of Art in 1987 and a recipient of the Chartered Society of Designers Annual Medal in 1989. He is summed up by his archivists at the University of Brighton Design Archives as a 'nonconforming, irreverent, idiosyncratic, strong-minded and talented problem-solver' – a 'character', but a Colossus in the world of exhibition design.

Robert Yorke Goodden, 1909–2002

...a tall, shy, charming, vaguely patrician man with an enormous breadth of erudition and a great human sympathy.
Fiona McCarthy

Goodden is largely remembered as being the evangelical Professor of Silversmithing and Jewelry at the Royal College of Art, championing design

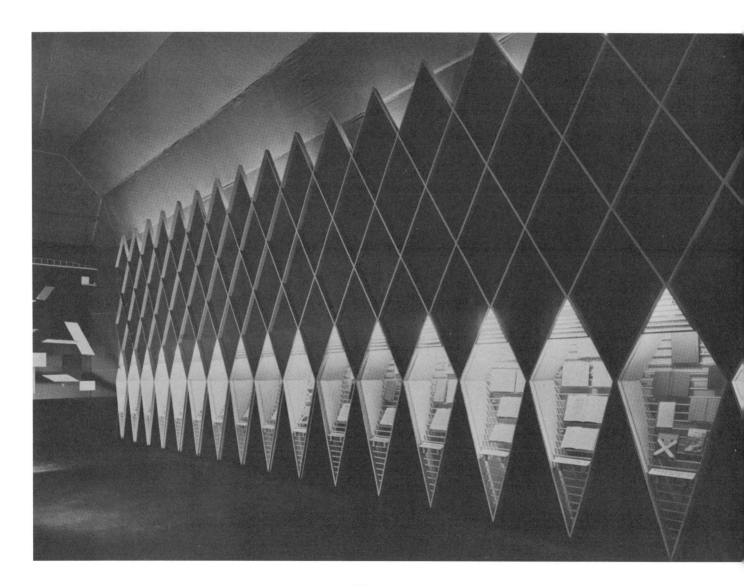

using metals. Fiona McCarthy, who was certainly in the know as her husband, David Mellor, had been a student of Goodden, claimed in her obituary for him:

There is still hardly a metal worker in this country not touched at some point by the Goodden influence.

It is possible that Goodden may never have got involved with exhibition design as an outlet for his talents and source of income but for his meeting up with the likes of Richard Guyatt and R.D. Russell when he worked in camouflage in WWII, for there is no record of his taking part in exhibition design before the war.

Goodden had, in fact, trained as an architect at the Architectural Association, from 1926 to 1931, but had begun to interest himself in product design as architectural commissions were slow to come in in the inter-war years. He ran his own small design company – Asterisk – that produced wallpaper, and he had begun to establish himself as a glass designer, producing designs for mass-produced glass for the Chance Bros., as well as starting to take commissions for design in silver.

Goodden's first exhibition work was for the 'Britain Can Make It' exhibition of 1946, where he was part of the team built up by Spence and

Gardner. He designed part of the Leisure Section, four large poles, mounted with material, with various sports equipment, from tennis to shooting, displayed at their bases. McCarthy wrote of it – 'His surrealistic montage of the British sporting instinct still strikes me as a brilliant design'. His work for the exhibition seems to have led on to other commissions, as for 'Enterprise Scotland' with stands for the Scottish Furniture Manufacturers and for the Scottish Cooperative Society. Much of this he did with R.D. Russell, with whom he was, by then, in partnership, although his striking wall of diagonal display spaces for the Printing Section is accredited to him alone.

From around 1947 through to 1951 he acted as consultant architect to the Board of Trade for the British Industries Fairs, as well as providing a number of stands for other exhibitions, as for the British Pottery Manufacturers in 1947 – a series of linked fair booths with an external mural by Laurence Scarfe. In 1950, Goodden's stand for the Furniture Manufacturers Association was rated, by *Art & Industry*, as particularly noteworthy.

By 1948 Goodden was installed as Professor of Silversmithing and Jewellry at RCA. He was commissioned by Casson to design for the Festival of Britain along with Russell (Professor of Wood, Metals and Plastic) for the Lion & Unicorn Pavilion, the name of which is said to have been coined by Goodden. He is personally accredited with the extraordinary flight of doves, the cartouches bearing quotations from English literature and the five model theatres displaying Shakespeare plays. McCarthy wrote of his contribution:

...he relished the concept of past illuminating the present and the resultant exhibition was clever, erudite, beguiling – and fun.

Goodden appears to have done little exhibition design after the Festival, albeit he and Russell provided some displays for the British Museum's Greek rooms in 1971.

Goodden received many accolades for his work in product design and design education: RDI (1947), Master of the Faculty of RDI (1959–1961), Warden of the Goldsmiths Company, Chairman of the Craft Council, and, of greatest pleasure to him, Pro-Rector of RCA from 1967 to 1974 (he was involved with Casson and T. Cadbury Brown in the design of the College's new building).

Richard Guyatt, 1914–2005

Richard Guyatt was, essentially, a graphic designer, Professor of Graphic Arts at the RCA for some thirty years from 1948 to 1978. That he got involved in exhibition work seems to have been largely his being drawn into it by others than IT being a specialist area he chose from pesonal interest.

Guyatt grew up in Spain, with a Spanish grandmother, and where his father was British Consul in Vigo. With no more formal art training than attending some of Bernard Meninsky's classes at

Left: Richard Guyatt's show card for the 1949 British Industries Fair, 'printed in three colours for distribution at home and overseas'. **Right:** Guyatt's exhibition display for the General Post Office, BIF 1948.

Westminster College of Art, before WWII he worked in a freelance capacity for advertising and illustration. In the war he was in Camouflage and it is there he met up with Hugh Casson, Robert Goodden and Robin Darwin. Darwin enlisted Guyatt's help when preparing a report on the future of the Royal College of Art, and, on being made Principal, as a new broom, swept away many of the old staff, and brought in some of his former Camouflage colleagues, including Guyatt. Guyatt found himself a Professor, at the leading design school in the land, from talent and personality alone, for he lacked the usual formal qualifications of someone climbing the academic ladder.

When Russell and Goodden got their commission from Casson for a pavilion for the Festival of Britain, Guyatt inevitably became part of the team. Casson, Goodden and Guyatt, in various combinations, had already done a little exhibition work through their association with Stephen Tallents' 'Cockade', as when Guyatt and Casson designed the Council of Industrial Design's stand for the British industries Fair, in 1947, and Guyatt and Casson for Wedgwood at the 1949 Fair; and Guyatt, and his wife, Elizabeth

Corsellis, again did work for Cockade for the 'Three Hundred Years of Catering' exhibition at the Tea Centre. Guyatt became a Director of Cockade and was, in fact, to write a chapter on model-making in Misha Black's book on exhibition design.

In his obituary of Guyatt in the Independent, Gerald Beckwith described him as 'one of our last remaining examples of a genuine Edwardian gentleman' and certainly Guyatt drew easily from the past to achieve the sense of history required for the Lion & Unicorn Pavilion, using what Darwin described as his 'ruminative imagination'. Amongst the various exhibits that Guyatt designed were the metallic Coat of Arms, the Cream of Poetry and English Language and the British Law section. To exemplify the cosiness of it all, Casson's wife acted as Guyatt's assistant. The Festival seems to have been Guyatt's last major contribution to exhibition design. He was to have a distinguished career in graphic design and in teaching, his services recognized by a CBE in 1969. He became Rector of RCA, retiring in 1982.

James Holland, 1905–1996

James Holland is, perhaps, best remembered for his work for left-wing causes, prior to WWII – playing a part in the start-up and activities of the Artists' International Association (AIA), and illustrating and providing satirical cartoons for publications as the *Left Review*. But for a period, in the middle of his career, he was involved in exhibition design, with AIA, with the Ministry of Information and the Central Office of Information, and at the Festival of Britain.

Born and brought up in Kent, he was educated at the Mathematical School in Rochester, and from there, he won a scholarship to the Rochester College of Art. In 1924 he went on to study painting at the Royal College of Art, where Paul Nash was one of his teachers, and James Boswell (later associated with him at AIA) was a fellow student.

On leaving RCA, Holland continued painting, showing at various London galleries, and earning his living as an illustrator for magazines such as *Lilliput*, and as a commercial artist, as well as doing political and anti-war cartooning. He worked for a time for an advertising agency which handled the Shell account amongst others. Holland, who had worked on the Shell account there, left the agency when the account was transferred to another agency and began to work as a freelance.

It was in these years, leading up to WWII, that Holland got his first experience in exhibition design, working along with Misha Black and others on an 'unofficial' Peace Pavilion that pacifist organisations had constructed near to the Trocadero entrance to the Paris Exhibition of 1937. Holland and Black worked on two of the Pavilion's rooms – those for the League of Nations, and for the International Peace Campaign. Part of his contribution was a mural – 'a compilation of statistics with lots of little figures and symbols'.

Artist's impression of the Festival of Britain touring aircraft carrier Campania, 1951, fitted out by James Holland as a mini-floating Festival that visited Britain's coastal towns.

But Holland was to serve his exhibition 'apprenticeship' during the war with the Ministry of Information and then with the Central Office of Information, becoming, eventually, Chief Designer, Exhibitions and Display. One example of his work, then, was a travelling exhibition to illustrate the work of destroyers, for which he had to visit Chatham Dockyards, where many of his relations had worked. He was to design another travelling exhibition, later, for CoI for 'The Cotton Show'. Holland continued to do government work through to 1949, alongside magazine and book illustration and some advertising.

It was in 1948 that he joined the Presentation Panel for the Festival of Britain. Whether chosen by him, or allocated to him, he was delighted, given his background, to work on the Sea & Ships Pavilion, and the fitting out of the aircraft carrier Campania as a mini-floating Festival of Britain, touring coastal towns. Holland had already been typecast as a shipping designer with his children's books commissioned by Noel Carrington – 'How They Sail', 'War at Sea' and, with his wife Diana John, 'Ships and Boats'. The Festival Pavilion was designed by Spence, with Holland having responsibility for the display within, which was to illustrate not only the history of British shipping and current shipbuilding, but also the fishery industry. It would seem that 'maritime' matters stayed with Holland after the Festival with his book designs for some novels on naval subjects for Cassell.

After his Festival work, for which he received an OBE, Holland returned to advertising, becoming Group Art Director for Erwin Wasey, with whom he worked through to 1963. Over the years he became increasingly involved with the educational and professional aspects of design. He became Head of the Faculty of Visual Communication (1963–71) at Birmingham Polytechnic, and then Education Officer for the Society of Industrial Artists, recording its history in a publication – *Minerva at Fifty* in 1980. In retirement Holland continued to paint and even ran an art class.

Described as a quiet, self-effacing man, he was nevertheless to make not inconsiderable contributions to the pre-war pacificist movements, wartime exhibitions, to art education and to his profession; as well as, for a period, to exhibition design.

William (Willy) de Majo, 1917–1993

De Majo was known as a prolific and ingenious packaging designer, a consultant to a variety of firms, and perhaps best remembered as a founder, along with Peter Kneebone, of the International Council of Graphic Design Associations (ICOGRADA).

He was born, of Yugoslav parents, in Vienna and studied at the Vienna Commercial Academy. This was with the plan to enter the family's textile firm, but, on doing so, de Majo found the work uninspiring and, in 1935, decided to leave and to set himself up in his own studio, to work as a freelance designer.

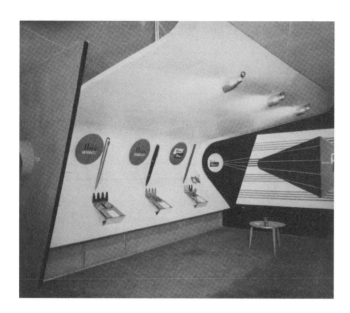

de Majo's stand for Biro writing instruments,
Miles-Martin Pen Co. Ltd., *c.* 1949.

With the onset of war he came to England, working
for a time with the BBC Overseas Service, before
joining the Yugoslav Air Force as a pilot in 1941.

At the end of the war, in 1946, de Majo returned
to commercial art, setting up W.M. de Majo & Assoc.,
one of whom was his wife Veronica, who worked
with him on a number of commissions. Two of his
major clients were in the drinks industry – W.A.
Gilbey's (distillers and vintners) and Clayton's (fruit
drinks), and along with these de Majo was a design
consultant to a number of firms, selling a variety of
goods, including John Millar & Sons (confectioners),
Miles-Martin Pen Co. (to promote BIRO), Miles
Aircraft & Henry Lunn Ltd., Charles Letts & Co. and
Blades & Nash Tyzock Industries. In addition to his
graphic design work (including packaging, stationery
and point-of-sale advertising), de Majo also designed
products (as glasses for Smirnoff Vodka and a table
with sunken drinks compartment for Gilbey).

The role of exhibition designer can also be added
to his list of achievements as he produced a number
of display stands for several different companies. His
most important exhibition commission was when it
was decided, somewhat belatedly that as the Festival
of Britain was to be a nationwide affair Ulster should
not be forgotten. De Majo had responsibility for the
overall conception of the 'Farm & Factory Exhibition'
which was mounted at Castlereagh. Although modest in terms of actual footage *Display* wrote of it:

*...in other respects, it conforms to the high
presentation standard of the larger more ambitious
promotions seen elsewhere, and has commendable
qualities all its own.*

De Majo had the use of a newly built, but yet to
be used, factory to which he added his own vertical
feature, a metal tower. The Exhibition told the story
of Ulster and its main industries – linen, shipping
and rope. Amongst the 'commendable qualities'
was the excellent captioning – 'impossible for any
visitor with reasonable intelligence to follow the
theme throughout the piece'. Because of the limited
space, the Ulster Exhibition played more on display

Willy de Majo's Farm and Factory exhibition held in Northern Ireland as part of the Festival of Britain, 1951.

themselves retained as designers for the General Design and Exhibition programme for Micron SA, Venezuela, but de Majo, showing his own work on the trip, conceived of an exhibition of a group of British designers to tour America. This he mounted in 1956 – 'Designers in Britain' – including, along with his own work, that of Abram Games, Hans Schleger, Misha Black, Ernest and Robin & Lucienne Day.

As with other émigré European designers, de Majo was international in his outlook and networking. He lectured abroad frequently and had set up an office in New York as early as 1948. He became Chairman of Icograda in the mid-1960s, and in 1969 the Society of Industrial Artists and Designers awarded him its design medal for 'International Services to Design and the Profession'; he was to receive similar awards from a number of European countries.

His archives are held in the Design Archives of the University of Brighton.

Beverley Pick

In his book on exhibition design, Misha Black claimed that it was a first; he was wrong for Sir Lawrence Weaver had produced a heavy tome as early as 1925, and in 1957 Beverley Pick produced another.

Very little is recorded about Beverley Pick, yet his name was attached to dozens of exhibition displays throughout the 1950s and well into the '60s. His book – 'Display Presentation, exhibition, window and outdoor displays' was illustrated largely from

strengths than architectural ones, which would have suited de Majo's experience to that date. Generally it was rated well-coordinated and on a scale appropriate to the community.

Art & Industry recorded, in 1952, that:

...an increasing demand abroad for the services of British designers in the planning of exhibitions is a satisfactory outcome of the 1951 Festival of Britain.

De Majo and his wife undertook a six week tour of North and central America, the Caribbean and the West Indies during which they not only got

148

his own designs; and he wrote a number of articles for the display press. He formed a company, Beverley Pick Associates, of which the most frequently named 'associates' were Neville Walters, Leonard Callow and Tim Sharman. Pick's consultancy, and another one of which he was a director – Sage-DCO, were involved in exhibition design and window display, along with shopfitting and product design. They not only designed light fittings but were responsible for various Regent Street Christmas decorations. It is not always easy to tease out exactly Pick's contribution to all this, but his name is always there.

James Holland refers to Pick as one of his colleagues at the Ministry of Information and he definitely designed for the Ministry's 'Victory over Japan' in 1945, as well as producing posters for its 'Jungle Front' and 'Army Signals' exhibitions. 'Victory over Japan' was held on a bomb site in Oxford Street and had, as its principal feature, an enormous hemisphere of canvas stretched over a frame, with hundreds of glass rods piercing the surface, designed to give a comprehensive picture of the Allies' movements against Japan. The sequence of lighting was synchronized with a recorded commentary.

From the late '40s Pick was regularly designing exhibition stands at both the Ideal Home Exhibitions and the British Industries Fairs (including stands for several Commonwealth countries who used to exhibit there), as well as for the Radio Show. Although he worked for dozens of different companies one of his major commissioners was BOAC, for whom

Left: Beverley Pick's exhibition stand for Bowaters, Packaging Exhibition, Olympia (undated). **Above:** Pick's exhibition stand for BOAC, *c.*1949.

he designed both window displays and exhibitions stands. One example, commented upon, was a combined stand for BOAC and BEA at a British Industries Fair, centrally placed, with no shell constriction, for which he decided to illustrated 'airiness' with a 30ft high construction, again with a globe, this time revolving slowly. Pick was prone to make use of height in his designs, as for those he designed for J.H. Birtwistle, the textile manufacturer. For a notable stand for the company at Earls Court, again in a central position, he constructed a tower covered with fabrics with rotating plaster cherubs below.

Many of Pick's stands were noted for their exceptional lighting, as when he used pendant reflectors through glazed openings of a ceiling for English Electric, or another ceiling he designed for BOAC made white with fluorescent tubes. Beverley Pick Assoc. designed a whole season of new light fittings for the General Electric Co. in 1954, which he described as 'unashamedly shiny'. He seems to have become something of a specialist on lighting generally, and wrote on the subject for *Art & Industry*.

Some of Pick's exhibition designing was for exhibitions abroad, as for a British trade fair in Baghdad, where he had to cope with display models broken in transit and local labour 'leaving much to be desired'. He produced a stand for Babcock & Wilson in an Atomic Power exhibition in Geneva in 1955, showing the history of the company with a model of Calder Hall, Britain's first atomic energy power station. Having 'shown off Britain' doing displays for its coal mining and steel industries for the Festival of Britain, Pick was commissioned to show off the 'Genius of Britain' at Expo 67, in Montreal. Pick had a three-dimensional mural of Britain's 'Great', a jet engine dividing the Rebels and Reformers from Parliament and English Liberty.

In his writings on exhibition design Pick seems constantly alert to possible differences of opinion between exhibitor and designer:

It is not always easy to strike a proper balance between the client's understandable desire to feature a maximum of information and the maintenance of simplicity and clarity of message, so very essential to good display.

As other designers, Pick used his exhibition work for experimenting:

All aspects of design find new expression and stimulus in the field of exhibition work, the average stand providing a test bed for new materials and new techniques.

In their introduction to Pick's book the publishers say that he was barely known to the public, appreciated mainly by his profession and his clients; certainly, in retrospect, he must be rated amongst a handful of outstanding designers who devoted most of their time to exhibition design, especially in the early post-war years.

Basil Spence, 1907–1976

I have always felt that far too much has been made of the problems of exhibition construction – the subject is simple. The conditions are ideal [usually indoors] and no architect who had a normal training need fear the adventure of pure design.

Basil Spence was the most Scottish of exhibition designers. Although born in Bombay, he was brought up in Scotland, began his architectural training there, kept an office there for a good part of his career and contributed to the major pre- and post-war Scottish Exhibitions – the 1938 Glasgow Empire Exhibition, the 1947 Enterprise Scotland, and the 1949 Scottish Industries Exhibition.

Basil Spence's exhibition display stand for ICI at the British Exhibition Copenhagen, 1948 (display design, Albert Smith).

Trained as an architect, and, indeed, best noted in architectural history for his design of Coventry Cathedral (for which he was knighted in 1960), Spence, nevertheless, carried out a considerable amount of designing for exhibitions. His initial training at the Edinburgh College of Art, was followed by evening classes at the Bartlett School of Architecture, University College, whilst working in the office of Sir Edward Lutyens in London. He returned to Scotland to build his own practice, doing some lecturing at his old college meanwhile.

Spence's first exhibition was in 1934, for the Edinburgh Architectural Association; but an altogether bigger challenge was for the 1936 Scottish Development Council's Pavilion at the Empire Exhibition in Johannesburg; and out of this work came Spence's major pre-war exhibition commission for the Empire Exhibition in Glasgow in 1938. For the main Glasgow Exhibition buildings Spence worked in collaboration with Tait, producing sleek, white low level silhouettes. Tait was attracted to Spence's rather dramatic modernist style, found him good to work with, and pesonally endorsed his election to RIBA. Brian Edwards described Spence's 'style' as 'blinding Scandinavian modernism' combined with 'Scottish romanticism', providing an appealing balance of the progressive and the traditional. Spence's ICI Pavilion for the Exhibition made use of towers of remarkable construction, the three linked together by metal tubing, and illuminated with coloured lights, the three representing the raw materials of the chemical industry – earth, air and water.

Curiously, with such notable achievements, Spence was not drawn into the maverick pool of exhibition designers at the Ministry of Information during the war, but found himself working in Camouflage,

Architectural drawing for Basil Spence's British Pavilion at Montreal's 'Expo 67'.

which nevertheless would have challenged his ingenuity and developed his technical knowhow.

Immediately after the war ended Spence was appointed Exhibition architect to work along with James Gardner as Chief Display Designer for the 'Britain Can Make It' exhibition in 1946, for which Spence was awarded the OBE. This was to be followed soon after by Spence taking a similar role for 'Enterprise Scotland', whilst, at the same time, acting as adviser to the Board of Trade for its British Industries Fairs (from 1947 to 1949), by which time he was working on his contribution to the Festival of Britain! The responsibilities he had for the Festival's Sea and Ship Pavilion, the Nelson Pier and the Skylark Restaurant necessitated his setting up a London office.

Through much of the 1950s Spence was immersed in his designing of Coventry Cathedral, and, in the '60s, with his appointment as Professor of Architecture at the Royal Academy, as well as taking important architectural commissions at home and abroad. Nevertheless it was in the '60s that he again tackled a major exhibition assignment for the British Pavilion at 'Expo 67' in Montreal. Spence not only had overall responsibility for this, but advised on choice of the designers for the various sections. The result was impressive; Edwards described it as a 'massive piece of sculpture with a big strong silhouette'.

It is significant that Spence's chapter in Misha Black's book on exhibition design was 'Construction Methods and Materials'. The last sentence of this links his architectural to his exhibition designing:

...it should not be forgotten that exhibitions are fundamentally the forcing house for experiments which will no doubt take on a more solid form at some later date.

Whether he was designing single exhibition stands or exhibition pavilions. Spence was continually experimenting, trying out new materials and new forms of construction – cupro-nickel tubing for ICI at the Empire Exhibition, translucent cloth draping cone-shaped towers for 'Enterprise Scotland', exposed steel framework for Babcock & Wilson stands, and later, for the Festival, further permutations on 'towers'.

Spence was picked out, in *Art & Industry*, for his outstanding contribution to the Empire Exhibition (1938), particularly for his ability to design equally well for exteriors and interiors. And this was acknowledged, some twenty or so years later, when the RSA attributed his RDI election to 'Exhibitions and Interiors'. Spence was to become something of a popular figure, with his later broadcasting and lecturing, and he was to make significant contributions, not only to the Royal Academy and the RIBA, but to such causes as the Civic Trust. Although he will be best remembered for Coventry Cathedral, the Hyde Park Barracks, and similar monumental buildings, it was his exhibition designs that initially got him recognition and gave him the opportunity to test out, on a small scale, what he was later to make use of on his grander, more permanent structures.

Sir Lawrence Weaver, 1876–1930

An exhibition stand is simply a form of advertising. It may be a poster in the round, it may be a supreme effort of shop-window dressing, it may be a sales counter, but it is advertising all the time.

There needs be no excuse for including at the end of this section a piece on Sir Lawrence Weaver, for although he was not a designer, he probably did more than anyone else to advance the design of exhibitions in this country in the 1920s. Without any formal education or training after leaving school, and with a life cut short by a heart attack, he nevertheless managed, by his skills of communication and organization, and by his patronage, to bring a degree of 'modernism' into Britain's traditional pomposity, when it came to 'exhibiting ourselves'.

A Bristol boy, his early career was 'on the road', selling firstly for an architectural fixtures and fittings firm, and then for an iron foundry. During this period he developed a strong interest in architecture, and began to write on a variety of architectural subjects. By his early '30s he had built up a sufficient reputation to be appointed Architectural Editor of *Country Life*, in 1910, and, as such, he also edited the Country Life Library – books relating to subjects covered by the magazine. Over the years Weaver was to write some ten books himself, on a wide range of subjects from 'leadwork' in 1909, and 'memorials and monuments' in 1915, to 'Sir Christopher Wren' and 'High Wycombe Furniture', both in the 1920s; and even one written with the help of Gertrude Jekyll, on *Gardens for Small Country Houses* (1914); most of these were published by *Country Life*, even after Weaver had left the magazine. In 1925 he wrote the first text on the subject of exhibition design *Exhibitions and the Art of Display*.

Weaver left *Country Life* to become a civil servant, at the Board of Agriculture and Fisheries. There seems to be no account as to why he was appointed to be Director of the British Empire Exhibition of 1924–5, but presumably because of the breadth of his knowledge and his administrative skills. He later recorded his contribution to the Exhibition as threefold – to introduce modernism, to have displays designed by professionals, and to bring some overall unity to exhibition design.

Weaver described his evangelism for modernism as 'a fertilizing stream from outside'. Practically immediately he was appointed he was off to exhibitions in Europe to see what he could cull – Munich in 1922 and Gothenburg in 1923. He recorded that attending them brought him 'sustained pleasure' and that he toured them 'without fatigue'. He received much criticism for espousing European aesthetics and described how he thought the opposition saw him:

EXHIBITIONS
AND THE ARTS OF DISPLAY

By Sir
LAWRENCE WEAVER
K.B.E., F.S.A., Hon.A.R.I.B.A.
Director : United Kingdom Exhibits,
British Empire Exhibition

1925
LONDON
COUNTRY LIFE LTD.
20 TAVISTOCK ST., COVENT GARDEN, W.C. 2
NEW YORK : CHARLES SCRIBNER'S SONS

The title page from Lawrence Weaver's *Exhibitions and the Art of Display*, the first text published on the subject in London, 1925.

He was demonstrably a light-minded fellow, almost certainly a Bolshevist and more than probably an atheist.

And of his determination to raise aesthetic standards of exhibitions by employing professional designers rather than contractors, he wrote of his critics' scoffing such highfalutin ideas:

...to use an architect for an exhibition stand, for an affair of stick and rag, of paint and matchboarding, was obviously an extravagance to be depreciated, if not an imposition to be fought.

The architects he turned to for the British Empire Exhibition were Westwood and Emberton. At first he commissioned them for a couple of stands, and then a few more:

...each less architectural in the old decorative sense and more architectural in the new expressive way than the last...

With Westwood and Emberton, Weaver achieved both modernism and professionalism at the same time, and this was a step forward in his more general campaign to bring 'real beauty' to design. Some records have Weaver being knighted for his handling of the Exhibition, but he must have been rewarded in advance for the Exhibition handbook has him entered as Sir Lawrence Weaver.

The unity he sought for exhibitions he was to achieve more effectively as Chairman of the Advertising Exhibition Committee in 1927, for the industry's show at Olympia. Of what he had found on his earlier trips to the Continent he had written:

...my eyes and mind were soothed by the seemliness of the setting. I believe that the outrageous weariness that has been regarded as inevitable in ordinary exhibitions in England is partly the result of the air of garish muddle that invests them.

For tackling the 'garish muddle' that could possibly imbue the 1927 Advertising Exhibition, Weaver turned to Emberton, who was now running his own practice. Weaver's concern for 'unity of design' was described as 'heroic', pursued with military precision, and achieved by having most of the stands of standard design, and then merely rented out to individual exhibitors, rather than let each exhibitor have a freehand in how they would show. Weaver triumphantly wrote:

Witty form and arresting colour take the place of richness derived from using those costly and permanent materials which give to Jacobean umbrella stands their cloying sweetness.

At the end of his book, where he sums up what he hopes will be the key aspects of future exhibition designing, Weaver fairly succinctly gives his recipe – more coordination, better artists, direct planning, clear vistas, standard elements to stand construction, variation of colour, appropriate lighting (not like Piccadilly Circus), and movement (working parts) – a shopping list that would stand as well to-day as it did then.

EPILOGUE

What hope can there be for the exhibition, which now seems to us what it has no doubt been all along, a heavy expenditure of time, money and effort for sometimes quite improbable results.
Milner Gray, 1952

The 20th century saw the flowering and decline of the exhibition as a medium of communication, whether to sell, to educate or to persuade. The exotic palaces and pavilions and fairgrounds, particularly prevalent in the international exhibitions, laid out over acres of land, dwindled to a mere handful of annual trade shows. The early melee of idiosyncratic styles had increasingly given way to a degree of central control and standardization, both in the overall design of exhibitions and in their constituent displays; flowers and frills and curlicues, as with architecture, been replaced by simplicity and strong lines. But just as exhibitions were becoming more professional, with architects and designers increasingly acknowledged, having exhibition design as one of their specialist interests, the exhibitors had begun to realize that it was all too much, that lavish expenditure and large visitor numbers in no way ensured a commensurate return.

Of course the collapse of the Empire precluded the pompous self-congratulatory exhibitions, masking reality; but, of altogether greater significance, was the rise of other more cost-effective means of advertising, of communicating, of informing – film and television, followed, towards the end of the century, by the internet with e-mails and websites and social networks. Nowadays specific messages can target specific recipients, wherever they are in the world. Nowadays, without leaving their offices and studios, merely by sitting in front of their screens and pressing keys, architects and designers can experiment as they will, when many had previously tried out, on the small stage of exhibitions, what they hoped, if successful, could later be applied more widely.

However, all is not doom and gloom for us exhibition enthusiasts, for many of these same architects and designers began to turn their talents for display to the challenge of museums; Gardner and Black were British pioneers in this field. Whereas, previously, few of the general public had had the courage to mount the ominous flights of stone steps to enter columned marble halls of the many grandiose Victorian edifices housing, frequently, the donated collections of wealthy eccentrics, and, if they did, were met with hushes from ushers to ensure a churchlike silence and religious awe, nowadays the all singing all dancing design, born of the exhibition, is making the driest of subjects accessible, even exciting. The queues once seen at White City and Wembley in the 1920s, on the South Bank in 1951, and at Olympia and Earls Court throughout much of the 20th century, now, in the 21st, wind their way along Old Brompton Road up Exhibition Road, and spread out into Great Russell Street. The eagerness for 'Exhibiting Ourselves', oftimes, in the past, providing great, if ephemeral design, whatever the motive, is still alive and well, it's just shifted site – to our screens, our mobiles, and our treasure houses.

REFERENCES

1925 Lawrence Weaver, *Exhibitions and the Arts of Display*, Country Life

1932 Wareham Smith, *Spilt Ink*, Ernest Benn Ltd.

1932 *Art & Industry: Report of the committee appointed by the Board of Trade under the chairmanship of Lord Gorell on the production and exhibition of articles of good design and everyday use*, HMSO

1937 Nikolaus Pevsner, *An Enquiry into Industrial Art in England*, Cambridge University Press

1946 intro. Herbert Read, *The Practice of Design*, Lund Humphries

1950 ed. Misha Black, *Exhibition Design*, The Architectural Press

1953 Richard P. Lohse, *New Design in Exhibitions*, verlag fur Architektur

1955 Michael Farr, *Design in British Industry*, Cambridge University Press

1957 Beverley Pick, *Display Presentation: Exhibitions, window and outdoor displays*, Crosby Lockwood & Son

1969 John & Avril Blake, *The Practical Idealists: twenty-five years of designing for industry*, Lund Humphries

1971 Dorothy Goslett, *The Professional Practice of Design*, B.T. Batsford Ltd.

1976 ed. Banham & Hillier, *A Tonic to the Nation: The Festival of Britain 1951*, Thames & Hudson

1977 John Allwood, *The Great Exhibitions*, Studio Vista

1978 Donald Knight, *The Exhibitions – Great White City, Shepherd's Bush, London*, Barnard & Westwood

1983 Rosemary Ind, *Emberton*

1984 Avril Blake, *Misha Black*, The Design Council

1984 Knight and Sabey, *The Lion Roars at Wembley – British Empire Exhibition*, Barnard & Westwood

1985 Raymond Plummer, *Nothing Need Be Ugly*, DIA

1986 Avril Blake, *Milner Gray*, The Design Council

1986 ed. Penny Sparke, *Did Britain Make It? British Design in Context 1946–86*, The Design Council

1993 1907–1995, *The ARTful Designer*, James Gardner

1995 Brian Edwards, *Basil Spence 1907–1976*, The Scottish Arts Council

1997 ed. Maguire & Woodham, *Design and Cultural Politics in Postwar Britain, The Britain Can Make It Exhibition of 1946*, Leicester University Press

1997 Deborah S. Ryan, *Ideal Home through the 20th century*, Hazar

2000 Jose Manser, *Hugh Casson: a biography*, Viking

2001 Lesley Jackson, *Robin & Lucienne Day: Pioneers of contemporary design*, Mitchell Beazley

2003 Becky E. Conekin, *The autobiography of a nation: the 1951 Festival of Britain*, Manchester University Press

2007 Paul Rennie, *Festival of Britain* (Design Series), ACC

2007 ed. Long & Thomas, *Basil Spence: Architect*, National Galleries of Scotland

2010 Trevor May, *Great Exhibitions*, Shire Books

2011 Henrietta Goodden, *The Lion and the Unicorn, symbolic architecture for the Festival of Britain 1951*, Unicorn Press

2012 Scott Anthony, *Public Relations and the making of Modern Britain: Stephen Tallents and the birth of a progressive media profession*, Manchester University Press

2012 Harriet Atkinson, *The Festival of Britain: A Land and its People*, I.B. Taurus & Co.

2013 pref. Paul Liss, *British Murals & Decorative Painting, 1920–1960*, Sansom & Co.